We're
Better
Than
This

Elijah Cummings

WITH JAMES DALE

Foreword by
SPEAKER NANCY PELOSI

HARPER
An Imprint of HarperCollins*Publishers*

We're Better Than This

MY FIGHT FOR THE FUTURE OF OUR DEMOCRACY

HarperCollins books may be purchased for educational, business, or sales promotional use. For information, please email the Special Markets Department at SPsales@harpercollins.com.

FIRST EDITION

Designed by Bonni Leon-Berman

Library of Congress Cataloging-in-Publication Data has been applied for.

ISBN 978-0-06-299226-0

20 21 22 23 24 LSC 10 9 8 7 6 5 4 3 2 1

To Baltimore—the city of Baltimore and
people of Baltimore.

To my parents, Ruth and Robert Cummings Sr.

And to our children, the living messengers to a future we
will never see.

Contents

Foreword

By Speaker Nancy Pelosi

"WE ARE BETTER THAN THIS!" In the summer of 2019, Chairman Elijah Cummings's resounding, righteous words thundered down from the Committee on Oversight and Reform hearing room and shook our nation to action.

During the height of the Trump Administration's barbaric child separation and incarceration policy, its top immigration official had been brought to explain why tens of thousands of children had been separated from their families. At the time, little children were sleeping on concrete floors, forced to eat frozen or inedible food, and denied basic sanitation. They were denied justice in court: babies who hadn't even spoken their first words were forced to show up in court to defend their immigration status.

The son of Baptist preachers, Elijah understood that every person contains a spark of divinity which makes them worthy of dignity and respect—particularly our children, who are, as Scripture says, a gift from God. And in the hearing room, when faced with evasions and mistruths, Elijah responded with towering moral clarity to remind those in charge that they were not meeting the needs of America's children.

Chairman Cummings's forceful statement helped ignite a movement to protect the children and defeat the Trump Administration's inhumane child separation and incarceration policy. And, for many Democrats in Congress, it would become immortalized as our moral mantra: an unflinching challenge to us all to go forth in a way that is worthy of the oath of office that we take to the Constitution, worthy of the vision of our Founders, and worthy of the aspirations of our children.

In the House, Elijah was our North Star, a leader of towering character and integrity. In his twenty-three years in Congress, he appealed always to our better angels, and to the promise of America. He brought to the House a voice of unsurpassed moral clarity and truth, calling the Congress to our principles and to a higher purpose.

Elijah's moral force and commitment to justice were critically needed during the Trump Administration, which was characterized by its culture of corruption, criminality, and incompetence. As the chair of the Committee on Oversight and Reform, Elijah used his gavel to protect and defend our Constitution's system of checks and balances as our Founders envisioned, shining a bright light on the administration's wrongdoing.

He worked to restore integrity and accountability to Washington, so that government would be a force for good for working people, ensuring that all could experience the American Dream, as he did. Indeed, Elijah's life's work was to open the doors of opportunity for others. He was committed to opportunity, the future, and the American dream because he had lived it. His story was the story of America: a son of sharecroppers who became Master of the House.

He defied discrimination, racism, and poverty throughout his life, confronting the segregation and bigotry of his childhood with a spirit of strength and hope. Elijah, long told that he could never become a lawyer, overcame these false limits, rising to become a respected attorney, be elected to the Maryland House of Delegates, and then be elected to represent the people of Baltimore and the Baltimore area in the U.S. House of Representatives. He intimately understood that he had a responsibility to make a difference; that to whom much is given, much is expected.

That sense of responsibility to help others fueled his decades-long fight to lower health-care costs, which is why House Members decided on his passing to name our prescription drug price legislation H.R. 3, the Elijah E. Cummings Lower Drug Costs Now Act. He lived in the same house in West Baltimore for more than thirty years, and he was always touched by the stories he heard in his community—particularly about the toll that high health-care costs took on families' economic security and well-being. He also saw this challenge through the prism of his own personal health challenges.

And that responsibility was why he fought to create good-paying jobs in Maryland and build the infrastructure of America as a senior member of the Transportation and Infrastructure Committee. As a member of the U.S. Naval Academy Board of Visitors, he took great pride in Maryland's role in our national security. He had so much pride in Baltimore—something that we shared and that made our work fun.

As he was Master of the House, working to create opportunities for all Americans, he was also Mentor of the House, opening up opportunities to younger and newer members. We all knew Elijah as a deeply generous leader, who always shared credit and took the time to mentor younger members, both on his committee and throughout our caucus. I remember how, during the first weeks of the new Congress, when members were being added to his highly coveted committee, he said to me, "Send me as many freshmen as you can." He wanted to help them succeed— and he wanted to learn from them, too.

Firm in his principles, Elijah was also a peacemaker and a bridge builder: passionate about what he believed in, dispassionate in his judgments about how to proceed. His clarion voice would cut through conflict, calming the waters and reaching out across the aisle, no matter how rough-and-tumble the debate. His friendships with members on the other side of the aisle were called "unlikely" by those who didn't know him. But those who knew him understood that it was values and patriotism that mattered to him, not party or politics.

Elijah knew that life was fleeting and precious; it was imperative for him to make the most of his time on Earth. The year of his death, he proclaimed, "When we're dancing with the angels, the question will be asked: In 2019, what did we do to make sure we kept our democracy intact?"

Elijah's leadership truly strengthened America, and his life and legacy will continue to inspire us all to go forth in a way that is truly worthy of the oath of office that we take to the Constitution, worthy of the vision of our Founders, and worthy of the aspirations of our children. For, as he often said, "Children are the living messengers we send to the future we will never see."

In Congress, we miss his wisdom, his warm friendship, and his great humanity. In Baltimore, we miss our champion. God truly blessed the United States with the life and leadership of Elijah Cummings.

What a blessing that, with this wonderful book, generations of Americans—our "living messengers" to the future—will now be able to read his words and learn from his beautiful life!

And in times of turbulence and uncertainty, may we all remember Elijah's moral charge: "WE ARE BETTER THAN THIS!"

We're Better Than This

Introduction

by James Dale

I don't often write an introduction. I am the "and" or "with" who collaborates with the well-known or highly accomplished person, the name in smaller type beneath the principal author. My job, my craft, is to help capture and convey the thoughts, experiences, and, most of all, the voice of that lead author. Not anonymous, but far from the spotlight, behind the wall so to speak. It is only in this uncommon circumstance—the principal author, Congressman Elijah Cummings, tragically died as we were completing the work—that I feel it is warranted and enlightening to take readers behind that wall. It literally sheds light on the story we are telling in this book. Elijah is no longer here to offer the reader a glimpse inside the background, determination, and process of telling his story. So, I will try to do so . . .

I began working with Elijah Cummings early in 2019. His wife, Maya, contacted me to explore the possibility of my helping him relate and share his story. He had long been contemplating sharing his life story and was finally ready to do it. He and I met, a sort of cautious first date to see if we connected. He asked me question after question after question about the process. How did it work? What role would we each play? How do publishers work? Editors? Agents? I didn't yet know that questioning, digging, gathering information, relentlessly probing like a courtroom lawyer was intrinsic to what made Elijah a social and political force. I asked him what he wanted his book to be. He said he wanted to leave a story for young people, especially disadvantaged young people, to show them what is possible. He also told me he was in a hurry. He wanted to get his story out in front of people soon, very soon. I also didn't know then how much of a hurry he was in, or why.

I told him that writing a book like this takes a commitment of time and he was a busy man with a huge burden and onerous schedule in Washington. Did he have time to write a book? He said, "Jim, I will make the time. I will make it." There were two telltale Elijah-isms in that response. First, he said my name—Jim—for emphasis, to make sure I heard him. He did that with family, friends, and everyone he worked with. If you heard your name, you knew he was telling you something important. Second, he repeated himself—"I will make the time. I will make it." There was a cadence to his speech, the child of preachers, that made his words memorable. That first meeting demonstrated his commitment to the book we hadn't yet agreed on or found a publisher for. He had scheduled an hour for me, but he kept me there for hours longer. He told me story after story. I was hooked on Elijah Cummings. Finally, three and a half hours later, we set our next meeting.

In the next session he told me more stories. I began to formulate a structure in my mind, a quilted interweaving of the formative moments of his past—as the child of sharecroppers, living in segregated neighborhoods, struggling in school—forming the fabric of everything he was able to do in later life—in Washington, in Congress, with presidents. The past informing the present and future.

Near the end of that session, we dealt with the delicate next step: Was I the right one to tell his story? Who else did this kind of work? Should he interview others? It was an invitation to sell myself. I didn't. I said, yes, there were other qualified, talented writers out there and his story was so compelling, he would have no trouble finding a partner. I offered one piece of advice: No matter who you choose, make sure you feel comfortable telling your story to that person, comfortable that person hears you and can capture your voice. He hardly paused, and said, "I'm comfortable with you. Let's go." And we began.

From then on, we met or talked every week, often several times a week, often early in the morning and/or late at night. When I look back at my calendar, I see that week after week, month after month, we had session after session of an hour, or two hours, or three. More than thirty individual sessions, plus multiple hours of research and background per subject, plus interviews with key people in his life, plus writing and rewriting and rewriting again. In terms of sheer math, it would be hard to calculate the number of hours we logged together. We met at his office in Baltimore. We met at his office in the Rayburn Building on the Hill. I rode back and forth with him from D.C. We had countless email exchanges. And even more text messages, often sent or read late at night or early in the morning. I could never wake up earlier than his most recent text.

I sent him excerpts and sections, first the proposal for publishers, then revisions. He told me, "I like it. It sounds like me talking." Later, I reviewed sections with him in conversation: "This is what I'm writing up now." He'd say, "Did you include the story about such and such?" "Yes, I did." Or, "No, tell it to me . . ." "Did you talk to so-and-so?" "Yes, and he told me the story you suggested." I delved into areas that were personal and sensitive. His family life. His first marriage. His children. Finding his soul mate in Maya. God. Race. Republicans. Each time we explored delicate territory, he would say, "I don't know if I want to talk about that." And I'd say, "Congressman, remember that this is your story. Why don't you tell it and see how it feels." He'd say, alright, starting out tentatively and then, little by little, letting out more and more, willingly, often relieved to unburden himself. He would reveal moments and feelings he'd never shared before. Each time, after hearing himself open up on a sensitive subject, he would reflect for a moment and say, "Okay, let's tell it. Yeah, I should tell it." He once told me that talking to me was "like talking to a shrink." It was a compliment, I'm pretty sure.

Over almost a year, Elijah Cummings shared stories he told before, but now with more intimate detail; he delved into new areas he had been reluctant to explore, he shared his hope and his fears for the country. Finally, he revealed the perilous state of his health. First a little, then more and more. I began to realize that he was in a hurry to tell his story because he was not well, much sicker than almost anyone knew. Still, he believed that as he had done in the past, he would manage somehow to survive and go on. Those around him had that same belief based on past rallies. But this time he did not escape his fate and he died in mid-October 2019. It was an abrupt ending. As weakened as he was, confined to a hospital bed, he had kept working, on government matters and on this book. The first week in October, I suggested we have our next session in his hospital room instead of on the phone and he agreed, but he later opted for a call. We spoke for over an hour. The following week, we texted. Late on the night of October 16, I sent him a text reading: *"Congressman, I am working on a section leading up to and into impeachment process. Would like to talk when you have a few minutes." Wed. Oct 16, 11:10 PM.* Congressman Cummings died at 2:45 a.m. on October 17, less than four hours later. That morning, when I looked back at my text feed, below my last text it said: *Read 10/17/19.* He was engaged to the last. In a hurry to the last.

Fortunately, due to his determination and his relentless drive, we had gathered and chronicled a full picture of his life, through notes, recordings, interviews with family, friends, and colleagues—the unique, uncommon, and inspiring story of Elijah Cummings. Unfortunately, while he saw sections of the manuscript as they were drafted, he was never able to see the entire assembled manuscript. Maya was there to the very end. Maya and I worked diligently to make sure that this book was true to his vision and his wishes. And it is in her words that we are able to tell the final chapter of his story. Personally, this book, this project, this work behind the wall, was the most meaningful and indelible experience of my writing life. I am grateful for the opportunity that he and Maya gave me. I believe generations will be grateful for the story he has left them. As he wished, it is a legacy for future generations.

Pain, Passion, and Purpose

"I am humbled and honored to be the next chairman of the primary investigative body of Congress."

Those were the words I uttered the first day of the 116th Congress. On January 4, 2019, after the Democrats won back the majority in the House of Representatives, I had been named chairman of the Committee on Oversight and Reform. More than "humbled and honored," I was determined to pursue the actions that had been so necessary since the day Donald Trump took the oath of office.

It is the job of the Committee on Oversight and Reform to "oversee"—inspect, supervise, keep an eye on—and "reform"—improve, rectify, mend—that is, to find the truth and hold those responsible to be accountable, and I looked forward to it. After twenty-four months of the Trump presidency, there was a staggering mass of allegations warranting investigation—collusion with foreign governments, interference and tampering with the election process, business deals that broke campaign finance rules, payments of hush money, conflicts of interest, improper security clearances, an attempted Muslim ban, attacks on the FBI, veiled and overt personal threats, and dangled pardons.

As we began our work, even more disturbing behavior, unworthy of American ideals, came to light—separating families at our borders, turning back asylum seekers, virtual acceptance of white supremacists, flirtations with dictators, rejection of allies, hostile trade wars, a revolving door of important government positions. Throughout it all, the president unleashed a barrage of inflammatory and bullying tweets, while any and all unfavorable stories about him and his businesses, family, and administration had been labeled "fake news."

As we embarked, I had no idea how hard it would be to do our job, to what lengths the White House would go—the denials, disregard, and disdain for law and justice, suppression of evidence, defiance of subpoenas, twisted facts, attacks on perceived enemies, and outright lies—to prevent the American people from learning the truth. But that resistance and obstinance only strengthened my resolve. Indeed, my story is one of overcoming, of moving through the obstacles in front of me. Everything I'd accomplished had been building toward this final test, and with the gavel in my hand, it was here.

I was ready.

I'd spent a lifetime preparing for this moment, a lifetime striving to help others. I grew up in South Baltimore and arose from those streets to the U.S. Congress. I'm a Democrat—but more than a party, I believe in people, in freedom, in opportunity, in country, and in making sure we have a democracy to leave our children. I've spent most of my adult life serving the public because I believe that is why I was put on this earth. That may sound lofty but it's what I feel to my very core. I have a recurring dream where I see myself running down a street lined with people. One person shouts out, "I need a blanket," and I hand him a blanket. Another says, "I need a cane," and I hand her a cane. "We need food." "We need shoes." As I run down that street, I hand each person what they need. I just keep running and running. To help others rise up—to find food, shelter, clothing, hope, and truth. That is my purpose.

I am the child of sharecroppers (post–Civil War servitude— black people "renting" farmland from white landlords that they could never afford to pay off) who came north for a better life. Neither had much education; my father did hard labor at a chemical plant; my mother cleaned white people's homes; at eleven I was a kid integrating a pool; in school I was labeled special ed. But I went on to graduate Phi Beta Kappa, earned my law degree, and was elected to the Maryland General Assembly and then to Congress, now in my twelfth term.

In spite of, and because of, where I've come from and what I've been through, I am an optimist. Some might say too much of one. I was one of the first Democrats to meet one-on-one with President Trump after his election. I brought him an idea I thought was good for everyone—rich, poor, Democrats, Republicans—lowering prescription drug costs. He said he liked it and that he'd go to work on it. Instead, he went silent, and soon turned his back on health care altogether. But that incident gave me insight into Donald Trump that would prove to be very valuable.

At a time when division is more prevalent than unity, I have done my best to act without anger or hate. My work philosophy is simple—to be effective and efficient. To find common ground, I connect with adversaries—I do not think of them as enemies—including staunch Republicans Trey Gowdy, Darrell Issa, Jason Chaffetz, and Mark Meadows. We may disagree on 85 percent of the issues, but I see the 15 percent we can work on for everyone's good.

Now I'm the chair of the Oversight Committee and we're involved in investigations into issues that are quite literally threatening our democracy—Trump-Russia connections, Trump's taxes and finances, the Mueller Report, immigration and border policy, family separations, and racism. I am taking on some of the greatest challenges in our nation's history. I am seeking to do the right thing at a time when doing the wrong thing is verging on becoming the norm, on becoming acceptable. It is *not* acceptable. I will do my best to stay positive. I will call on the lessons learned throughout my life to guide me. We will find the truth. But I will do my job. I remind people on all sides: do not mistake my kindness for weakness.

In the Bible, Elijah was a prophet—a messenger of God's

word—a humbling burden for a man to carry. While I do not consider myself a prophet, I have tried my best to listen for God's instruction and speak truth even when the truth isn't popular. I have said many times, "We're better than this . . ." I said it on the streets of my home, Baltimore, a city on the verge of explosion over police treatment of citizens. I said it in Congress when microphones were shut down, barring free speech. I say it now when the president flaunts his power and ignores the Constitution. I say it when he resorts to bullying, name-calling, and feeding racial divisions. We are better than this. I will continue to say it. Because we must call out what is wrong, and call on our better selves to make things right. This is a fight for the future of our democracy.

All that I have done, all that I have built, has been the prelude to where I find myself now.

Some years ago, I came face-to-face with my own mortality, a life-threatening battle. I do not complain. It happened for a reason—to make me hurry, hurry to do the work I was put here to do, in the time I have been given. My pain fuels my passion; my passion drives my purpose. I am running down that street to help all the people lined up on the sides as fast as I can.

I believe there is an arc to each chapter of our lives, and those chapters all come together to create a larger arc—the story of our purpose and progress over a lifetime—and maybe even a legacy.

CHAPTER 1

The Lie and the Lesson

I met with Donald Trump in good faith. Then he lied to me. It was one of hundreds, then thousands of lies Donald Trump would tell, not only to me but to the country and the world. But I didn't know the scale of it yet. None of us did. And if anyone had told us, we all would have said, that's impossible; he's the president of the United States.

In January 2017, I became the first Democrat to meet privately with the new president. I met with him with genuine optimism. Caution, yes. But I had faith—an important word for me— that two people from opposite worlds and worldviews—a son of sharecroppers, who couldn't even own property, and a real estate billionaire and reality television star—even people who fundamentally disagreed, could accomplish good things. I still believe that. But I don't believe it's possible with this man, this president. Here's how it started, back when I had that glimmer of hope.

First, I received my invitation to President Trump's inauguration—every member of Congress gets one but not everybody goes. I thought to myself, this guy, whether I like it or not, is going to be the president of the United States for four years. And I've got to represent 700,000 people, no matter what. I don't know exactly what this president and I can do together, but if there are things that we can agree on, I want to get them done for my constituents and for the country.

So I decided to go. But with all the tension in the air, I knew I could get a lot of criticism for attending. Right then, Trump was in a dispute with a good friend of mine, Georgia congressman and civil rights leader John Lewis. I went to John and told him that I wanted to go to the inauguration but would never do anything that looked like I was disrespecting him.

"No, Elijah, you should go," he said to me. He understood exactly why.

With his blessing, my wife, Maya, and I went. We were also invited to the luncheon in Statuary Hall after the swearing in, an invitation that we hadn't received even under President Obama. We were seated at a table with some of the president's family, and listened to remarks from the president, Vice President Mike Pence, and other dignitaries. During a lull in the program, we walked up to the head table to greet President Trump, who said, "I'm really glad to see you." I guess that was partly because he thought Democrats, and especially African-Americans, would stay away. There were very few of either group in the room. I used this time to talk about an issue that was very important to me, the high cost of prescription drugs the pharmaceutical companies were charging. The president agreed and said, "They're getting away with murder, those companies." That's a quote. He said he wanted to sit down and talk about what we could do. Honestly, I was surprised, but I saw it as a sign that maybe we could do something together.

Not long after, I did get a call from the president—directly from him—that he wanted me to come to the White House. We set a date, but I had to cancel due to a conflict. (Later Trump would falsely claim I said it was because "it might be bad for me politically.") Nonetheless, we rescheduled and met in early March, which, as far as I know, was the first meeting he had one-on-one with a Democrat. I asked Dr. Redonda Miller, president of the Johns Hopkins Hospital, to attend as well as Congressman Peter Welch of Vermont; both are advocates of prescription drug price reform.

Surprisingly, meeting with President Trump, we had what seemed to be a wonderful conversation. The person I am, the person I've always been, came out. And I *thought* the real him came out, too. I knew I was sitting with the president, but I didn't feel like I was sitting with the president. I live in the inner city of Baltimore, and I'm used to people being very straight with me, no games. And that's how we talked . . . or so I thought. I don't know whether it was me being naïve, but I felt like I could reach him, that there was a level of mutual respect. He asked me why I was so personally concerned about prescription drugs. I can remember my words. I told him I'd seen too many people die because they simply couldn't buy their medicine. It's like you put a gun to somebody's head when they're sick, and they've got no money, or not enough money. They could be making $150,000 a year. Then somebody tells them they need to buy a prescription that costs $1,000 per pill to stay alive. I know people who have faced that. And then they've got a hell of a choice: Do they take away from their families so that they can stay alive? Or do they say, no, I can't put that burden on my kids or my wife or my husband, and then they die?

As I was telling him that story, a tear came to my eye.

"That's a real tear?" Trump said. I nodded. "You're not like Schumer, are you?" he asked (because he had infamously accused Senator Chuck Schumer of crying fake tears).

"Yeah, Mr. President, it's real, man. This ain't bullshit." I said it just like that. I felt like I was talking to a guy on my street, not like he's the president. Just man to man. That's how we talked.

I told him about the legislation Congressman Welch and I had worked on to enable the federal government to negotiate prices with the pharmaceutical companies the way they do with Medicare. The president said he liked the idea and turned to Tom Price, secretary of health and human services, and said, "Let's get it done." Price, who as a member of Congress had voted over and over to repeal the Affordable Care Act, looked at him, I'll never forget the expression on his face, as if to say, *You must be kidding.* But he said, "Yes, Mr. President."

I thought, well, that's a pretty good start; it's time for me to go. But Trump wanted to keep talking, so we did, just the two of us. I took the opportunity to get a few more things off my chest. First, I asked him, "Mr. President, why do you say things that are so mean?" And I went on. "The Muslim ban," I told him. "You don't need to do that. It seems like you're representing just the people that like you. Mr. President, you should represent everybody. When you talk about the African-American community, when you call these areas 'shitholes,' when you talk about African-Americans like we're all doing bad, like we're all in the ditch and can't get out, and we live in murder capitals, I wish you wouldn't do that, because it hurts us."

He looked at me and said, "You really mean that, don't you?"

"Yeah, I mean it," I said. "Mr. President, you're almost seventy, man, and I'm sixty-seven. It won't be too long from now that you and I will be dancing with the angels. Why can't we join together and get some things done, like prescription drug prices, that will affect everybody and be good for everybody? If we're able to do something like this, I can tell you, if you could, you could become probably one of the greatest presidents that ever lived." I started with "if"—*if* he could do something like this— and that was a big if because it meant he'd be doing something for everyone, not just his base, who would probably follow him to the end of the world. All he had to do was try to help the other people.

He said he liked that, and as I left, he told me he'd be in contact with me very shortly.

Two or three days later, I got another call from the president. He told me, "Congressman, I'm working on this thing. I'm going to see what I can get done." And I was hopeful, truly hopeful. What if we really started something positive?

Then after that, I never heard from him again. He turned his back on the prescription cost idea and instead went after the total repeal of Obamacare. That's when I realized that he doesn't mean what he says; he says whatever he feels like at the time, and whoever he talks to last is who he believes. It was then that I realized he's not a guy from the neighborhood. He's not a guy who's straight, whom you can trust.

But that doesn't mean I stop fighting. I'm just getting started.

WHO AM I? What drives me? Where do I get my resolve? What am I made of? These are questions we don't often ask ourselves. They're hard to answer. We have to look inside.

I'm made of those who came before me—my parents and grandparents—of those who surrounded me—my brothers and sisters—the places that shaped me—the streets I grew up on—and the lessons I lived and breathed without even knowing it.

My parents were sharecroppers who left South Carolina and came north to Baltimore looking for a better life for themselves and their kids. Neither had more than an elementary school education—they could read and write but they never learned complicated math, science, or geography—and until they came north, they never had indoor plumbing. But they taught us more than any teacher or class or school. They taught us with values and wisdom and experiences that never left us.

The wisdom I gained from my parents was rooted in their own upbringing as well. I never knew my grandfather but my father told me about him. My father was maybe eight years old, living in Manning, South Carolina, poor as could be but smart as could be; nothing got by him. His father was a preacher (like my father became when he grew up and moved to Baltimore).

One Sunday, the grandfather I never knew was giving his sermon in the pulpit. And in the midst of preaching, he didn't feel well. Whether he'd been ill for a while, nobody ever knew. But this day, in front of his whole church, he got weak. He grabbed on to the pulpit but then he fainted and fell down. Members of the congregation rushed up to him and tried to comfort him but he was gravely sick. He didn't come around. So they lifted up his limp body and put him in a wagon and pulled it down the dirt road to his little house. My father and his brothers and sisters ran alongside. My father said his mother, my grandmother, held my grandfather's hand all the way home.

Somebody had been sent to town to get a doctor to come to the house, which they did in those days. Folks from the church put my grandfather in his bed and tried to make him comfortable. Finally, two doctors came by, both white, one younger and one older, and they went in to examine my grandfather. My father had to leave the room and wait on the porch, but he could hear most of the conversation. The doctors checked out my grandfather, poking here and there, feeling for fever, doing what doctors do. Then they walked out of the room together to discuss his condition and what to do.

The young white doctor said to the older one, "Doc, we have to get this man out of here," no doubt to a hospital or clinic, someplace that had better facilities and treatment. He said, "If we don't get him out of here, he's going to die."

The older doctor said, "Don't worry about him. He's only a nigger."

My father, age eight, out on the porch, heard it all, even though they were whispering. "He's only a nigger." He's not a person.

He's something less, someone who can be allowed to die. Without care, without treatment, he could die. In those days, they didn't have heart surgery, but they had diagnostic tools and heart medicines, things that might help. But he didn't get any of it. Because he was only a nigger. And that night, he did die.

When I was growing up, my father would tell me that story, and no matter how many times he did, it was always just as painful for him because he knew those doctors didn't value his father's life. My father used to say, "Lord, give me three score and ten of life." I didn't know what a score was when I was a kid but my father got more than that. He made it to seventy-three. That story of my grandfather never left him. My father became a strong advocate to make sure his own children and his whole family had proper health care. And the story never left me, either. I thought, that's not right—somebody has to do something.

As a young kid, I learned that lesson all over again, this time with a sliver of hope. I got a job working for "Doc" Albert Friedman at Onnen's pharmacy in our neighborhood, doing whatever Doc said needed doing—unloading inventory, stocking shelves, and delivering orders. People came in for their prescriptions and Doc knew each one of them by name. He knew their medications and he knew what each one was suffering from. He knew how important those medicines were to each of his neighbors. And he knew sometimes they didn't have the money to pay for the prescriptions. So he just gave the medicines to them.

It wasn't good for business to give medicine away and could cause Doc Friedman personal trouble. But Doc thought you'd have worse trouble if you didn't get the insulin for your diabetes, or your blood pressure pills, or penicillin for your child's infection. He'd ask you to pay for it when you could, if you could, and plenty of times he never saw the money. He knew the moment he gave them the medicine that he likely wouldn't be repaid. But he knew some things were more important than money. Somewhere in the back of my mind, I kept that story, too.

Then over and over and over, year after year, I saw those stories repeat—grandparents dying, children suffering, families who can't afford medicine, people hurting. I saw it in my neighborhood, in my city, in the whole country. Many times, I've had voters come up to me and tell me about an aunt who died because she had no insurance, a cousin who couldn't get an operation, a mother whose child died for lack of an antibiotic. I went to church and prayed for people who couldn't afford to see a doctor, or go into an emergency room, or buy a pair of crutches. I got letters and emails and folded-up notes, of terrible, awful, tearful stories that just should never happen. And I kept thinking, somebody has to do something. Somebody has to do something.

That conviction is what I took into my first meeting with President Trump. I took one more thing: the words of my grandmother. Just before she died, she said to me that for too long white people had been telling African-Americans to wait—wait until things got better, wait for changes, wait and things would improve. We've been waiting since we were brought to this country as chattel, since slavery ended, since Reconstruction, since the civil rights movement, since Kennedy and King and Johnson and Clinton and Obama.

She said, "Your daddy, he's been waiting and waiting for a better day. He's going to wait and he's going to die." She said to me, "Elijah, don't you wait. We cannot wait anymore."

I realized that we have been stopped from becoming all that God meant for us to be. I don't have time to be patient.

I CARRIED ALL of that into my meeting with the president. And I carried much more.

I carried what my parents gave me. My father did low-wage, manual labor at a chemical plant where the bosses gave the black workers the jobs that white workers wouldn't do. My mother took the bus each day to clean houses of white people living in the nicer parts of the city and then came home to raise her seven children in a small row house in South Baltimore. They each worked all week at these lay jobs, and then on weekends, they preached. They formed their own church that went through a series of names and temporary locations before finally becoming the Victory Prayer Chapel in its own home near where we lived. I grew up in a house that was very religious. You couldn't dance or play cards. My mother lived to age ninety-two and never wore makeup a day of her life. We had to adhere to strict religion seven days a week. In reality, they preached all day, every day, in every room of our house, without calling it that. We were raised not just by two parents, but by two preachers. They gave us a strong moral foundation and taught us how to live.

Over the years, I've been asked why, given my background and values, I didn't become a preacher. People say I speak like a preacher, with that rhythm, cadence, and passion. I often use the words of the scripture. I look to God for guidance. I have, on occasion, even acted as a preacher. I performed the marriage of *Morning Joe*'s Joe Scarborough and Mika Brzezinski. Joe is a former Republican congressman from Florida and Mika is the child of Zbigniew Brzezinski, national security advisor to Democratic presidents—once again, a case of my reaching across the aisle to join people together.

But my answer to why I didn't become a preacher is that, by the example I saw growing up, you must be perfect, a truly perfect person. That is what I saw in my parents. I am far—very far—from perfect. I am human, flesh and blood, passionate and vulnerable, and I think that enables me to reach out to others with human weakness and needs and help them. I can only strive to follow my parents' example. I can only strive to do good.

I remember when my father worked at Davison Chemical (later owned by W. R. Grace), usually working the swing shift, 7 a.m. to 3 p.m. He did brutal, backbreaking work, hauling drums, cleaning vats, carrying heavy loads, and getting filthy every day, the demeaning labor the foremen knew they could not get white workers to do. Black men did those jobs. And I remember that every day when he came home from work—we lived in a little row house near where Oriole Park is today—he had a ritual after work. He'd park his car (he was one of the few in my neighborhood who had a car and owning it was a point of pride) and sit in it and not come in the house. No matter how cold it was in the winter or hot in the summer, he'd just sit there, quietly, all by himself, in a world of his own. For a full hour. We kids wanted him to come in but we knew better than to bother him. Years later, I learned what he was doing out there. He told me he was letting the day's indignities pass, allowing the anger and the pain to diffuse, giving the venom of insult and disrespect time to leave his body and his mind before coming inside to his family. He would not bring that negativity or bitterness into his home. That was not forgotten by me.

Later in life, I wrote him a letter because I wanted him to know, before he left this earth, what his example meant to me. I told him that he was the most important figure in my life, providing for our family as best he could, never raising his voice to my mother. I told him I wanted to live my life as well, and as fairly, as he had. We talked about what it was like at that job at the chemical plant, and he described the way he was treated, the disregard, degradation, and insult.

"I was called everything but a child of God," he said to me.

That's why he sat in his car. That's why he let the poison drain before facing his family. To this day, I try not to let an insult or affront prevent me from dealing with adversaries. I sit in my car, figuratively not literally, so many times a day or a week or a year, and that enables me to pursue sometimes seemingly impossible tasks.

Like my father, my mother had very little formal education. But she was probably the smartest person I ever knew. One of seventeen children, she did whatever she needed to do to get by, to help her family and then our family. She took long bus rides out to the grand homes of Guilford and Roland Park, and she cleaned those homes, took care of those children, and prepared their meals, for $7.25 a day. Then, at the end of an already long day, she came home to our house and did the same tasks for our family. She passed on profound lessons as casually as putting dinner on the table or wiping a dish or waving to a neighbor. Lessons just came out of her naturally. Not arithmetic or biology but life lessons. I can still hear her voice saying, "You teach people how to treat you." When I first heard that I thought, what does that mean? I can't make someone be nice or give me respect or return my phone calls. Or can I? Maybe by the way I treat them, the way I act and react, what I say, whether I'm polite or demanding, kind or unkind, holding them to high standards, maybe I can teach people to do right by me.

In fact, my mother taught me how to act in the United States Congress. In one instance, her lesson gave me everything I needed to handle what turned out to be not just a political issue but a personal offense; some might even call it abuse. I had to handle the person who had inflicted it, Republican congressman Darrell Issa. At the time, Issa was the chair of the House Committee on Oversight and Reform (the committee I now chair—turnabout sometimes comes). The committee was in the midst of hearings looking into conduct by the Internal Revenue Service and whether they had improperly targeted conservative nonprofit groups. We had a witness on the stand and the chairman and other members had asked a lot of questions and made their statements. I had one more statement to make. But Congressman Issa decided we had all said enough, learned enough, and he abruptly ended the hearing. He would not allow me to speak. That was bad enough. That was disrespectful to me as ranking member, or to any member. But worse than that, he stood up, said "we're adjourned," and shut down the mics. Then he did something in an instant that sent a cold chill through the room. He gave a slash-across-the-neck motion—some called it a lynching gesture. Still, I tried to speak even without a microphone, to say this is not the way any member of Congress should be treated, not the way the government should work, or the way we should conduct a democracy. But I couldn't be heard. That was hardly the end of it. Democrats and some Republicans immediately reacted to Issa's gesture, calling it an ugly reminder of ugly history—the Ku Klux Klan, self-styled justice, racism, killing people by hanging them from trees. A motion was proposed on the floor to condemn him for that act. I did not join that fray. I let the others do it. But ultimately the motion was not passed.

Of course, the media jumped on it. Issa and the slash, the hate and bigotry it conjures up, were on every nightly news report. I did not add to the fire. I only addressed the need for everyone to be heard in the democratic process. Then the Congressional Black Caucus called for Issa's removal as chairman of the committee. Not too much later, I got a call directly from Darrell Issa. He apologized to me personally. Then, he told the press, "As chairman, I should have been more sensitive to the mood of what was going on, and I take responsibility."

But what happened up to that point was only half of my mother's lesson. The other half came up shortly after. There is a tradition in Congress that the portrait of each chairperson is hung in a formal ceremony. All members of the particular committee are invited to attend. It was time for Darrell Issa's portrait to be placed. But the pain of the slashing gesture was still fresh. Should I attend the ceremony? Should I refuse? A day or so before it was to occur, I spoke to my then-eighty-five-year-old mother. I told her I wasn't sure what to do. She said, "Elijah, absolutely you should go. This man made you famous."

She was not only telling me that you teach people how to treat you, she was showing me exactly how to do it. You must act better than the other person. I took her advice. I went, I even spoke, and in my speech, I quoted my mother telling me to go, telling me that Darrell Issa, in his way, had made me more prominent. From that day on, Darrell Issa treated me with the utmost respect. I would even say we became friends. We were almost always on opposite sides of issues, but as equals in search of answers. I've invoked that lesson from my mother over and over through my career and my life. Not just with Darrell Issa, but with others across the aisle—Jason Chaffetz, Trey Gowdy, even Mark Meadows, Tea Party member and founder of the right-wing Freedom Caucus. Folks have referred to my relationship with Meadows as an "unlikely bromance." I personally advised both Chaffetz and Gowdy, in their frustration and despair over the president's behavior, sometimes taken out on his supposed allies, that they are still young men and don't need this poison in their lives. They both have since retired from elective office and I don't take personal credit for their decisions, but I do know we confided in one another. Despite our differences, we taught each other how to treat each other. I only hope my mother's wisdom can help me with Donald Trump.

I LIKE TO say I am a man of faith—not blind faith, but spiritual and human faith. When I was born, we belonged to the Mount Moriah Baptist Church, made up of mostly people like us, from South Carolina. One of those people was Maggie Woodlaw, a friend of my mother, who became my godmother. In those days, people from the church often helped a family raise the kids, because nobody had much, but together folks could help take care of each other. Maggie, my godmother, was the one who told my mother and father to name me Elijah. She'd read the story of Elijah in the Bible—the prophet and miracle worker in the Old Testament—and felt that name was somehow fitting for this new little baby. When I was little, I hated the name. Kids would tease me, singing the old song, "Oh Eliza, little Eliza Jane . . ." As a young boy, I would have preferred a plainer simpler name like my brother James or my father, Robert . . . anything but Elijah.

But later I came to appreciate it. I went to church and read the biblical stories. Elijah stood up for the worship of God over the pagan deities and God performed miracles through Elijah, one of which was said to be raising the dead. Elijah appears in the Old Testament, the New Testament, the Talmud, the Quran, the Book of Mormon, and Baha'i scriptures—a messenger of God to so many people. Elijah wasn't a plainer, simpler name. It carried real meaning. In fact, the name Elijah is a humbling burden to carry. I am not a prophet. I do not perform miracles. But I try to live up to my name and legacy, to bring about change, to make people's lives better.

Today many people just know me by Elijah, my first name. They don't know me as Mr. Cummings or Congressman, just Elijah. They call out to me on the street. They send letters addressed, Dear Elijah. They greet me in church or on my way to work. They do not see me as a prophet but as someone who cares about them. Am I a messenger of God like Elijah in the Bible? That's not for me to say. I attend church every week that I am able. But God is not a once-a-week activity for me. I am, in every sense, spiritual. I feel I can discern the spirits of other people. If I cannot feel someone else's spirit, I tend to keep my distance. When I do feel it, I am drawn to those people. Each morning,

I follow a ritual of listening to gospel music, which grounds me and helps me prepare for the day. I pray for guidance, meditate on what to say, and then speak according to what I believe God has said to me. I try to do what God has told me to do.

I am a man of great and abiding faith in the spiritual and religious sense, but also in the personal, hopeful, human sense. I have faith that things can get better. If . . . *if* . . . we put together the will and ideas and intentions to make them better. And if we don't, no amount of faith will fix things.

My pastor today knows me well. Bishop Walter Scott Thomas Sr. is more than my pastor; he's my friend, and has been for decades. Bishop Thomas leads the New Psalmist Baptist Church, with a congregation of over seven thousand. He is a remarkable man, studying economics at the University of Maryland when he was called by God to serve, who went on to earn his master's and doctorate of divinity, who not only heads the congregation, but has a nationally broadcast television show, *Empowering Disciples*, and has written several books. Bishop Thomas is a charismatic, brilliant, sensitive man who has the rare ability to connect with people of all religions, ethnicities, and backgrounds. I brought President Bill Clinton to New Psalmist once and he felt so at home, he was so taken with Bishop Thomas and the church that he not only attended the service but stayed for the meal that followed, and then hours afterward, and was still engaged in conversation with Bishop Thomas, to the point that finally we had to gently urge him to go home, go back to Washington, D.C. That is the powerful effect Bishop Thomas has on people, his ability to connect and bond with them.

The pastor knows me so well that he knows I have been a loner for most of my life, a bit of a contradiction because though I reach out to, and affect a huge family, an entire community, there are only a very small number of people I will let get truly close to me. Bishop Thomas is one of them. I trust him. And I do not trust—deeply trust—many. But once you've gained my trust, and I know I can depend on you, we are friends for life. That's what I have with Bishop Thomas.

To me, there are two types of trust, or two levels: One is about honesty and integrity. Is the person genuinely honest and does the person act with integrity? If the answers to both are yes, then maybe that is a person to trust. Maybe. The other type of trust is, does the person do what he or she says they'll do? It seems that should be simple. If you say it, do it. But so many people don't do what they promise. They ignore their own words. Intentions may be good, but results matter. The ones who deliver, who do what they say, those people will never let you down. The first type of trust is special. The second is rare. And having both, well, that's almost an endangered species. It shouldn't be, but it is. Bishop Thomas, to me, is both. And I hope I am to him. I know I trust him with my life. He trusts me with his.

I have been in his church for thirty-seven years. For a lot of those years I was his lawyer and the church's lawyer. I worked for them on weekdays and prayed with them on Sundays. Then, when I went to Congress, I had to give up my law practice and I could not do their legal work. But the bishop and I could still counsel each other, seven days a week.

We all have our areas of expertise where we each lean on each other. When I hear him preach, it makes me want to be a better politician, to be as good at what I do as he is at what he does. It's like when I used to watch Michael Jordan play basketball—man, it was a beautiful thing to witness—and it made me want to be the Michael Jordan of the legal profession. It's like that when I see Bishop Thomas. It inspires me to be the best I can be, to be more than I thought I could be.

I turn to him for the spiritual, for inspiration and aspiration; he can turn to me for the political, for law, rights, and justice.

Not so long ago, he asked me who I was going to support as the nominee for president. I said I hadn't determined that yet. He said, when you do, tell me, because whoever you support, I support. "That—politics—is your church." He reminded me that when I got behind Barack Obama, way before he was even officially in the race, when I said this man was destined to be our leader, Bishop Thomas said, "If you trust him to lead, I trust you." I was the first person in Maryland, one of the first in the country, to come forward and stand with Barack Obama, and then others began to follow. That was hard for me because I was close with Bill Clinton and Hillary Clinton and I deeply respected both of the Clintons. But I had to make my stand. The bishop stood with me. His parishioners stood with him and he's known all over the country (and pastors all over the country, and their congregations, began to back Obama). That's trust. That's friendship. That's what the brother—and I do mean brother—does for me. I can count on one hand, outside of my family, the people I feel that way about. The pastor is one.

Together, Bishop Thomas and I walked the streets of Baltimore on that night in April 2015 when the city almost erupted after the Freddie Gray incident. Freddie was a twenty-five-year-old African-American who had been arrested by Baltimore police for allegedly carrying an illegal knife, was put into a police van, in which he somehow went into a coma, and then had to be taken to a trauma center. A few days later, he was pronounced dead; the cause of death given was injury to his spinal cord. There was immediate outrage. How could a healthy young man sustain such injuries in a van ride that would result in his going into a coma? How could his spinal cord be damaged on a short ride to a police station? What was the truth of what really happened? It was another unforgivable wrong in a growing list of urban human tragedies.

I was asked to deliver the eulogy at Freddie Gray's funeral and the words came from my heart. "To mother Gloria and to the entire family, I want you to know we stand with you during this difficult time." I looked right at that grieving mother and spoke to her one-to-one. "You brought him home. You played with him. You watched him grow. You heard the first time he read something. And you went to your own mother and said, 'That boy can read.' You just watched him grow." I touched my fingers to my lips to send love for Freddie to his grieving mother. Then I spoke to all the mothers and all the fathers about all the Freddie Grays. "As I thought about the [news] cameras, I wondered, 'Did anyone recognize Freddie Gray when he was alive? *Did you see him?*'" I asked that question "Did you see him?" because Freddie was like so many, hundreds, or thousands, or more young black men, who are invisible in our society. Expendable. Taken for granted. Seen only when there is a tragedy, an altercation, a police investigation, a news story. I repeated it, "*Did you see him?*" and then once more, "*Did you see him?*"

Three times. Because we do not see them. And we must. I picked up the memorial program and read from it: "It says Freddie joined the World Life Missionary Baptist Church in 2001, where he joined the youth line and was a junior usher. *Did you see him?* He loved church-sponsored events, the latest fashions, and sports. He played football with the Sandtown Wolverines. *Did you see him?*" I repeated it again and again. The question we must ask ourselves. I want the world to see our young black men and women. Now. Not when they're headlines, but when they're here and alive. I kissed my fingertips again for Freddie and his family. And I closed: "I've often said that our children are the living messages we send to a future we will never see. But now our children are sending us to a future they will never see." Angry and sad and heartbroken, I said, "There's something wrong with that picture." Why didn't we see him in life? Why don't we see so many in life?

After the funeral, I asked the public, the neighbors, the media for calm and for justice. (It wouldn't be until months later that his death would be ruled a homicide and several of the officers involved were charged with manslaughter. But legal actions against them later ended in dropped charges, mistrials, and acquittals.)

From April 18 to the 28th, the streets were full of angry, upset, untrusting folks. People marched. Crowds chanted. It was mostly peaceful, though highly charged. Some bricks were thrown. Some windows were broken. The city was on the verge of exploding. And no wonder. People felt they had been betrayed. The question was, what would they do with that anger and betrayal? The mayor declared a curfew of 10 p.m. Night after night, I went out into the streets trying to keep the peace. I understood that if one bullet was fired, the city could blow up. But I thought, and hoped, I could help keep the calm by talking to the police as well as the folks who could create some serious problems, because I personally know a lot of people; they're from my neighborhood. I live only five blocks away from Penn and North, an intersection that became the epicenter of the nightly unrest.

The very first night, I saw a man I knew, a young guy who was kind of a leader. It was about 9:30, only a little before the 10 p.m. curfew, and I said to him, "John, you need to go home." I could see he was mad; his eyes were on fire, he was agitated, walking fast through the crowds, shouting out, pent up, not sure where his energy would take him, powerful and maybe dangerous.

"Congressman," he said, "I'm not going home."

I told him I didn't want him or any of the people out there, people he might influence, to get arrested.

He said, "I can't do it, I can't just walk away. Even if they arrest me."

I was standing right next to him and I said the last time I saw him I remember him telling me he had two kids and a girlfriend, and a good job at the hospital. And that he took care of the kids at night when his girlfriend, their mother, was working. He nodded, yes, that was still the case. I asked him who was going to look after the kids if he got arrested. He said he didn't know but he had to be there, on the streets, right now, to deal with this unjust death.

I knew how he felt but I couldn't leave him there. So I wrapped both of my arms around him and hugged him. I whispered in his ear, "I love you. I do not want you to get arrested." I knew that even though he might look brave or bold, like a leader, in front of his boys, it wasn't going to help him or anyone in the whole community if he let his anger get out of control. I kept holding him close and I could feel the bulge of a gun tucked in his belt. I said, "You know if you have a gun and the police find it, you're going to jail tonight." And then everyone out there would get more and more agitated. Who knows how many others had guns. Who knows what could happen. Again I said, "I'm telling you this because I love you."

He almost couldn't believe it. He asked me, "What did you say?"

I repeated it again. "I love you."

He told me that I was the first man to ever tell him that. He said he sometimes felt like a man locked up in a casket, trying to claw his way out. He didn't feel a lot of love. He and his friends and neighbors, when something like the Freddie Gray thing happens, all felt caged and upset, thrashing out, looking for answers. I know how he felt. I think I know how all the folks out there felt. I promised him after this was over, I'd try to help him. And then I started singing—the spiritual "This Little Light of Mine"—quietly at first, and then building with more voices. "This little light of mine, I'm going to let it shine, let it shine, let it shine . . ." Then John joined me singing. And pretty soon he was helping get people off the corner, telling them to go home.

The next night, I was walking the streets again, and I saw John again. He came up to me and said, "Here I am, reporting for duty." He gave me a little salute and said, "We're going to make sure we get people home by ten." I asked him why he was doing this. I was glad, but I wanted to know what happened, and why. He said, "The first thing you did was you showed respect for me. And the second thing was, you said you love me." And he said there was something else, "That song . . . 'This Little Light of Mine.' I remember my grandfather, who'd been long dead, used to sing that song when I was a little boy in church." He kept going, ". . . I look at you as my grandpa, and I'm not going to walk away from my grandfather." That's faith. And trust. I cried. I face those situations all the time. Those moments are as important—maybe more important—than passing a bill in Congress. If you can reach one person, find a common path, then maybe, possibly, you can change outcomes. Whether it's a brother on the streets or politicians across the aisle. Trust. Just when you think it's not there, it can emerge.

IN THOSE TIMES when faith runs low—and it does for everyone—I sometimes turn to Bishop Thomas and he to me. I remember a time, a dark moment in his life, when he had doubt and worry and he confided in me (I would never reveal what it was because of the trust we share) and when it occurred, I told him, "Bishop, borrow some of my faith." He said he would. But I had borrowed that very phrase, that idea, from him. Because when I had doubts, or despair or worry—facing daunting odds of governance, or family tragedy, or threats to our democracy—when I was faced with challenges that I could trust him with, he said to me, "Elijah, borrow some of my faith." It isn't faith in God only, it's faith in the future, in turning the corner, in what could be . . .

That is what I found in Maya, my wife, my soul mate. This

part is hard to talk about. I'm a private person, especially when it comes to the woman who is the love of my life. My whole life, up to now and beyond. Eleven years of marriage, an eternity of connection. Bishop Thomas told me recently that he looks out at us in the congregation and he "sees a love that is rare." He said he sees it as we walk in and walk out, as we sit next to each other, the way we lean over and talk to each other, I guess things we don't even see ourselves. He talked to me about how she was set to run for governor of Maryland but then when I got sick and had to have heart surgery, she just walked away from that opportunity to be by my side. He saw all that. I didn't know he noticed it all. But he is right (as always); she is my best friend, and I am so fortunate to be married to my best friend, my very smart—book smart, school smart, life smart—best friend. (Forgive me but I would not do well married to someone not as smart.) Maya is *Dr.* Maya Rockeymoore Cummings and I am always the first to emphasize the "Doctor" title, a Ph.D. in political science, a policy consultant on issues of regional, national, and international impact, chair of the Maryland Democratic Party, well read, worldly-wise—that is some smart woman. And she is my soul mate. That isn't just an expression. It means she is my extra source of fulfillment.

The pastor says it's all right there to view. Our love and our connection. On view? Really? That almost embarrasses me. But I cannot argue with it; I just didn't know we were so obvious, like school kids. We do hold hands in church. In the words of Bishop Thomas, "she feeds Elijah's soul." She is with me everywhere, when she's there and when she's not. I hear her voice whispering in my ear. And if I don't pay attention, it's louder than a whisper.

I carried all of this—my grandfather's death, working with Doc Friedman, neighbors who couldn't afford their medication, my father's quiet resolve, my mother's lessons in how you teach people to treat you, my reaching out to adversaries, my voters, my church, my pastor, Freddie Gray, my wife, and my name—I carried it all with me into my meeting with the newly elected president, Donald Trump. I told the president if . . . *if* he could do something for everyone, not just his base; if he could lower the cost of prescription drugs . . . if he could do that for everyone, he *could* be a truly great president. He then turned his back on the idea. He went on an all-out attack on Obamacare. And then what did he do? He took my own words and twisted them into a lie, an ugly odious lie. He claimed I had said he would be one of our greatest presidents. No ifs, no coulds; he just claimed that I said *he would be one of the greatest presidents.* And he said it over and over, to as many microphones and cameras as he could find. Donald Trump told the *New York Times* that I said to him, *"You will go down as one of the great presidents in the history of our country."* I did not say it. He twisted what I did say into a lie. A flagrant, shameless, bald-faced lie. One of many. One of thousands, as it turns out.

One of the lessons of the street is that your first encounter with a person can tell you all you need to know. If a guy is straight with you, he'll be okay. If he isn't, watch out. I came out of that meeting, that entire encounter, with a disappointment, but a lesson in what we were now up against for the future. I came out ready.

CHAPTER 2

"The Lord Ain't Finished with You Yet"

If I wasn't driven enough on the crisis of health care and drug prices, I had my own crisis—a life-threatening incident—only a few weeks after my first meeting with the president. Maybe God was trying to tell me, "Hey, Elijah, this isn't just about other people. This is about you, too."

In April 2017, after a long day on the Hill, I felt like I couldn't catch my breath. I'd been working nonstop and just figured I was worn out. So I ignored it. Then it happened the next day and the next. Finally I mentioned it to my wife, Maya. She said, "Elijah, you're going to the doctor." I promised her I would when I had time but I had a packed calendar ahead of me. She said, "You're going now." So we went. That tells you a lot about me and a lot about Maya.

The doctor checked me out—the usual questions, poking, tapping, breathe in, breathe out, stethoscope, listening to my heartbeat—and I was sure he was going to tell me to take a day or two off, which I probably wouldn't do but maybe I'd cut my hours down for a while. But he didn't let me off that easily; he ordered an echocardiogram to confirm what he suspected. I was getting my day off whether I wanted it or not. The results were clear. I had "aortic stenosis," a narrowing of the aortic valve. It was cutting the flow of blood to the rest of my body and that's why I was short of breath.

I didn't like the news but I knew it wasn't a guess—I had the advantage of being in Baltimore; my doctors were at Johns Hopkins and they're the best in the world. I asked if it could get better on its own, with rest. No. In fact, it would likely get worse, narrower and narrower. Could I deal with it later, when my schedule was lighter? No. The sooner the better. But the doctor, Jon Resar (director of the catheterization laboratory and interventional cardiology at Johns Hopkins), said I was lucky. The condition is fixable. The treatment for me would be TAVR—transcatheter aortic valve replacement. It's noninvasive—that is, not open-heart surgery—going up through the femoral artery and implanting a new valve inside the old one. It's quick, proven, and recovery is fast. Effective and efficient—my work philosophy in a medical procedure. They scheduled me for the next day.

Okay, I thought. I'm taking a little vacation, even if it's forced, even if it's in the hospital. I'll get the valve and I'll be as good as new, maybe better. Maya said, "Elijah, you've got to hear what's being said here; you have to take care of yourself." She was right. But I couldn't help thinking, this is going to make me stronger than I was before. I could get even more done.

Still, I was realistic. I prepared two envelopes before the procedure. One was a list of people to contact if all went well, to tell them, don't worry, Elijah's fine, he'll be back to work soon, so don't let anything slide. The other was a list of instructions on what to do if things did not go well, if I was not around to tell everyone what to do—my wishes and funeral plans in detail. I called my chief of staff, Vernon Simms, and asked him to meet me and Maya at the hospital. He rode up in the elevator with us to check in and I took out the two envelopes. I gave the first one to him and told him, if everything went as planned, to open it after the surgery and contact the people listed. Then I asked him for a pen and wrote on the second one, "Maya," and I told Vernon to give it to her if things did not go well. She was standing right there seeing it all, but no one said a word.

I should say a bit about Vernon. He has been with me since the day I started on the Hill. He had been the chief of staff of my predecessor, Kweisi Mfume. I liked Kweisi and our views often coincided. Still, I wanted my staff, my own people, to start fresh with no allegiance to anyone else. But in those first days, I was almost overwhelmed with pressing matters of jumping into the job, a job I didn't know much about. So I asked this guy Vernon Simms to help me out, just for a few days, with no obligation to keep him on, in fact almost a promise that he wouldn't be staying. But he did too good a job. I came to rely on him almost immediately. I learned fast that I could trust Vernon with anything. And I do mean anything.

That included a time when someone stole my car in Baltimore and took it joyriding and partying. I didn't even know the car was gone until someone in my district spotted my government license plates and called to tell me where the car had been left, a pretty rough area of town. I asked Vernon to help me out. I gave him my extra car key and he and another staffer, Debra Perry, took it upon themselves to go down there and find the car. They called the police but the police took too long and the neighborhood was rough. They were surrounded by rowdy, loud folks, shouting about the congressman's car, taunting Vernon and Debra, probably scaring the daylights out of them. So evidently Vernon jumped out of Debra's car and opened my car door but the alarm went off and he was panicking, looking for the alarm kill switch. He finally found it, started the car, and took off with Debra right behind—the police never showed—and they returned the car to me. The only problem was, the police did have a report on it as stolen and a week later they pulled me over on the Baltimore Washington Parkway and I had to convince them I was Elijah Cummings and not the guy who stole Elijah Cummings's car. So, needless to say, I can trust Vernon with anything. Even my life. He took the envelopes and I knew he would do as I asked. (After things did go well, Vernon tried to give me the second envelope back for the next two years but I always told him to hold on to it.)

The following day, I had the TAVR. It takes a little over an hour, something like getting a stent. You come out of the anesthesia, spend a few hours in the ICU, and you're back in your room. The recovery is only a few days in the hospital, a few weeks at home. I was ready to feel better.

One day, not long after the procedure, I was in my hospital room, thinking about what I'd been through, when a woman, someone I didn't know, wandered in, calling my name, "Elijah! Elijah Cummings!" She said she had a message for me. "The Lord has been waking me all night and what he said was so important, I wrote it down." She reached into her blouse, pulled out a note, and read it: "He don't mean you no harm, he's just trying to get your attention. He wants you to know he ain't finished with you yet." And then she left.

I thought to myself, did I really see this? Was she here? But I was wide awake. I didn't dream it. It just happened. And I remembered the words so clearly. "He ain't finished with you yet." God really did have a message for me.

The doctors came in and checked me out and said the valve was working perfectly. Later that day, the nurses got me up and walking around. I was tired from walking but feeling very positive mentally. I'd be getting stronger every hour and back to normal fast, just as the doctors promised. But it didn't happen that way. The valve kept working but I was feeling tired, almost exhausted, not short of breath, but worn down and without energy. When I did walk, I was in pain, severe joint pain. It turns out, I had developed a serious gout infection. My feet were throbbing and pretty soon, I wasn't able to move. My two-day recovery stretched to weeks and months. Life slowed down. Work slowed down. But I had time to do something I didn't often do, to step back and think about everything.

Sometimes I'd replay the incident with the woman who visited me with the message. The Lord had certainly gotten my attention. Was God testing me further than I thought? When I would get a little down or negative about how slowly my progress was going, or the pain I was in, I'd think, well, this is all okay because at least he wasn't finished with me yet. Then I'd recall my own words to my children, neighbors, school kids, families in tough circumstances, colleagues in Washington, when misfortune visits: "Don't ask why this happened *to* me. Ask why this happened *for* me."

This health scare was there to tell me that our time on this earth is limited, finite, short. I was coming face-to-face with my mortality. I will not be here forever. We all know that is true eventually, but we don't want to think about it day-to-day. Most of the time, we shouldn't. We should be busy with the business of life. But sometimes we should take that step back, and take a hard look at what we were meant to do and how to do our best to get it done. This was happening for me, to tell me not to waste time on less important things or what couldn't be done and concentrate on what must and can be done. Now. The Lord wasn't finished with me yet. But he was telling me to hurry.

Hurry because, in the less than four months that Trump had been president, the threats and abuses to our democracy had been deeply disturbing. From tax cuts for the rich to destroying health care to a Muslim travel ban to unqualified cabinet appointees to racist dog whistles to enriching his own properties, to destroying the environment to pandering to Putin . . . and so much more. Yes, I have to hurry. Every day we don't do something, this president is whittling away our freedoms. Too many other people aren't hurrying. They're waiting for someone else to act. I have to hurry because I don't know how much time I have . . . or don't have. Hurry because our democracy depends on it.

But hurrying wasn't easy with my joints throbbing in pain. With the help of physical therapists, I pushed myself to walk. To go to my office. To go to Congress. To make calls and have meetings. To draft bills. To talk to colleagues. To get back to work. Without complaint. I started to feel a little better. I got around with a cane, or a walker. The important thing was to keep going. Gout was just an obstacle, one to overcome, and not give in to. And then one day I woke up and I couldn't move one knee. It would not bend. I forced myself up and out of bed. It was agonizing, excruciating, like something I'd never experienced. This time I didn't resist going to the doctor or the hospital. After a battery of tests, the results came back.

Sometime during my valve and gout recovery I had contracted a raging infection that went right to my knee, the patella, femur, and tibia. I was back in the hospital for treatment. The doctors performed two surgeries on my knee in an attempt to flush out the bacteria causing the infection. Days later, the infection finally started to subside. But the pain would not leave. The bones in my left knee were grinding against each other. I tried to will my knee to bend. It would not. With great effort I could push myself out of a chair, upright, leaning on a walker, shuffling it forward. After a few steps I was worn out. The doctors said they would have me see specialists, but in the meantime, I could go home.

If I felt up to it, I could go back to work. I did go back to work. But this time, in addition to a cane and a walker, I also used a motorized scooter to go from my office in the Rayburn House Office Building to the U.S. Capitol.

I did not feel up to going back to work. But in a way, it was my therapy. It focused my thoughts—do your job, help people, fight the fight, don't wallow in self-pity. Would I be able to walk again? I didn't know. But I was not going to slow down.

THE TRUTH IS, I had heard the message to hurry before. It wasn't only the heart valve or the knee or the gout. It was a more serious call that had come many years before. It was something that I find hard to talk about. I have mostly kept it secret throughout my life.

In 1994, when I was in my forties, I became very ill with a whole raft of symptoms, just agony all over. The doctors checked me out with every test imaginable and at first the diagnosis was elusive, mostly because what I had was so rare. It turned out to be thymic cancer, which is, frankly, almost always deadly. The cancer invades the thymus and prevents it from producing the white blood cells to fight infection. Medically, you just become a magnet for disease. The doctors told me the survival rate was low. They would treat me, operate on the primary tumor site, give me radiation and chemotherapy, and put me into drug trials, but I should approach life like I had a few months to live. So I have done just that, for more than twenty-five years. I've been under constant care at Johns Hopkins. I've been to the Washington Hospital Center for chemo and radiation. I've received treatment at the National Institutes of Health (NIH), with a drug intended for kidney cancer, that I responded to, at least for a while. The combination of treatments, the quality of medicine, the cutting-edge teams, the experimental drugs, have all helped to defy the odds, so far. I've outlived almost everyone else in the drug trials, almost everyone with this disease.

Ever since I got that diagnosis, I have gone about every day that way, as if I have only months to live. Only two years later, when I was elected to Congress, the very first speech I gave on the floor of the House was a recitation of a poem often quoted by Dr. Benjamin Mays (civil rights leader, president of Morehouse College, inspiration to Martin Luther King), fittingly titled "God's Minute" (attribution anonymous):

> *I only have a minute. Sixty seconds in it.*
> *Forced upon me, I did not choose it, but I know that I*
> *must use it.*
> *Give account if I abuse it. Suffer if I lose it.*
> *Only a tiny little minute, but eternity is in it.*

No, hurrying is nothing new to me.

I haven't beaten thymic cancer. I just fight it off every time the symptoms come back. And it is surely not finished yet. Nor am I. My pain is fueling my passion and my passion is giving me purpose.

I still hurt every day and sometimes, when I do, I call up the image of my mother. After a day of cleaning white people's houses, coming home and putting her feet in Epsom salt, singing her prayers the whole time, then fixing our dinner and making sure we had our homework finished, doing what had to be done for all of us, and going to bed, she got up the next day and did it all again. She didn't complain about her feet or her back or feel sorry for herself. She knew that wasn't why she was put here. She was here to raise a family and help people and her hurting body wasn't going to stop her from her purpose.

As long as I can remember, growing up, nobody in my family felt sorry for themselves. Now, that may seem strange. That doesn't mean things were always good. No, mostly they were not. My parents worked hard with two and three jobs. We didn't have enough money. Ever. Racial discrimination was a fact of life. But my parents knew that complaining didn't make it better. Doing something did. They lived by that belief and when both were called to preach, they built their churches on doing something, not wishing it so, or moaning about why wasn't it so. They said, and taught us, that when somebody needs help, you help. My father was one of the few people in the neighborhood who had a car, so he'd take people to the doctor or dentist or to apply for a job or to visit a relative. When someone in the neighborhood was pregnant, my mother would take care of them, and then help deliver babies, or take the mother to the hospital and look after the kids at home. We didn't have anything extra but we gave what we had and more. We gave money that we didn't have. That was the glue in our house—giving. And that meant feeling other people's pain.

To this day, one of my greatest strengths is to be able to feel other people's pain. But it's also one of my greatest weaknesses. How can it be both? I take on other people's pain as if it's mine. So, I hurt for them. I want to do something about it. I carry that burden.

If I cannot soothe their pain, I feel I have failed. Or failed so far and have to keep trying and trying. I go to sleep at night thinking of other people's pain. And sometimes I cannot sleep because of it. But it is what I do. I don't complain about it. I get up the next day and try to do something about it. Turn the pain into passion and the passion to purpose. My parents did God's work in the church. I try to do God's work outside the church.

We literally had no complaints in my house growing up—the house my parents bought for our family. Saving every dime they could, they finally managed to scrape together enough to buy a house in Edmondson Village, on Baltimore's West Side. It was a little bigger than the house we rented in South Baltimore and not too far away, but it was ours, our own home. They saved for it. They cut back on other things for it. They prayed for it. It was not only an American dream, it was an answered prayer. Owning a home was the reward of discipline—self-discipline, family discipline, faith discipline.

Discipline was never in short supply in our house. If you made a promise, you kept it. If you set your mind to do something, you did it. No matter how long it took. No matter what sacrifice it involved. You treated your family with respect, especially your parents. And if you didn't—either do what you said or show respect—there were consequences. When one of us kids was out of line, we heard about it, or worse, felt it. In those days, a whipping wasn't uncommon. You wouldn't do it now but back then, well, let's just say we learned fast to get back in line. In fact, after the age of ten, I don't remember any of us getting a whipping. By then we knew better. A look or a word from my father—the voice of God—was enough to get us in line. Discipline was not fear. Discipline was doing what was right. No one in the family was afraid to share anything with each other; our parents were open with us about everything.

So, when they got ready to buy the house—*our* house—my father told us about it and what it meant. They had been renting a small house and we were jammed in. He said any time they wanted to hang a picture, or paint a room, or lay down carpet or put up a front porch light—anything—they had to ask the landlord. He said they wanted their own "piece of America" and to "pass it down like white folks do." It wasn't just a house, it was a dream come true. They had achieved it with discipline. That meant sacrifices. He and my mother explained that for us to afford it, we wouldn't be able to get much that Christmas. Instead of resenting it, or complaining about it, we rallied around it. We were excited. We were proud. We wanted to be part of it. So my brothers and sisters and I (I wasn't more than ten) got together and decided to use all of our money from running errands and delivering papers and groceries to surprise our parents on Christmas with things for our new house. We didn't ask them what to get; we just went to a local place called John's Bargain Store and bought what we thought we'd need—lamps, dishes, bath mats. Then we hid all the presents at a neighbor's house until Christmas morning. Our parents were shocked; I mean they couldn't believe their eyes. That was a good Christmas and I think of the lessons from it. I also think that showed that my father was a natural leader, "leading" us to have our own home, and getting us to rally around it. I hope I get some of my leadership skills from him.

THAT CHRISTMAS WAS memorable but what happened and what it stood for was not out of the ordinary in my growing up. That's just how we lived as a family—for each other, with each other, learning from each other, protecting each other. My parents set examples for their children. My brothers and sisters set examples for me, and I did for them.

My older brother Robert Jr. was a huge reader, with walls of books, books, books. Reading books wasn't the most popular thing to do back then among kids of our age or where we lived. It wasn't that cool but Robert didn't care. He read and absorbed and learned about life beyond our block and our neighborhood. It rubbed off on me. I figured there must be something in those books worth knowing since they were taking up so much of my brother's attention. I didn't read nearly as much as he did, that would be almost impossible, but I learned where books could take you. Then he got a paper route to earn some extra money. So I did, too.

My older sister, Retha, taught me and looked out for me. If someone in the neighborhood was going to beat me up, she was my protector, always looking out for Elijah. You don't forget that. You store it inside and call on it later.

Robert became a lawyer; Retha and Diane are both nursing administrators; Carnel built a successful painting business; James was in the Air Force and now is in cyber security; my baby sister, Yvonne, does research on African-American breast cancer. My parents had very little education and modest jobs. But they lived a life that led their children to achieve more. To get the education they never had. To see where it could take us. And to be close to each other. That was family.

In our house, after God, came education. Right after God. But just because my family placed the highest value on education— it could transform your life—didn't mean it came easy to me. No, it was hard, arduous; I almost gave up so many times. When I was in grade school, I struggled and they put me in classes labeled "special ed." I realized very soon that "special" was another way of saying slow or behind the other kids or less demanding and definitely less interesting. Instead of loving school, I was frustrated, stymied, and discouraged. It was like wanting something that was just out of reach.

I guess my frustration showed on my face because I had a teacher—thank God for him—in the sixth grade who took me aside and said, "Elijah, you don't look happy sitting here in class. What's wrong?"

I let it all out and told him, "I feel like a caged bird, like I'm all locked in."

I was trying to say that I wanted to learn more, but I couldn't. The classes wouldn't let me. My abilities and learning up to that point wouldn't let me. The teachers wouldn't let me. I was trapped.

My teacher must have seen some potential in me because he tutored me and gave me a path to learn—books to read on my own, after school and at the library, exercises, and homework. It was hard, all my regular schoolwork plus the extra work. I spent hours, long hours, at the library, getting home late and doing more work. The libraries were the only integrated places in my neighborhood; the schools were all black or all white. And those late afternoons and sometimes into the nights, the mostly white librarians noticed me there and would come over to me, see what I was studying, and offer help. I didn't forget that—a lesson while doing my lessons—that there are a lot of good people of all colors. Sure, there are lots of bad people, people who will hold you back, but there are a lot of good people, people who care.

Little by little I began to catch up and pretty soon the teachers saw my progress. They moved me up to regular classes and I began to feel the rewards of school. It made a change in me—or rather that teacher and I did—that changed my whole life. I became literally hungry to learn.

I moved up to middle school and that was the first time I was in school with white kids. They treated me okay, especially the ones like me who wanted to learn. Of course, there were the kids, black and white, who would bully or beat up anybody who tried to be a smart kid. They would applaud ignorance and put down excellence. That phrase was something I said to myself whenever I saw it. It reinforced negatives and put down positives—don't study, be tough, talk tough; even people who spoke correct English were ridiculed. Kids would dumb themselves down to fit in.

This was echoed everywhere, by society, by movies, and by television. *Amos 'n' Andy* had been a popular series on radio—two white actors imitating and mocking foolish, poorly spoken, cartoonish versions of black men—and then it became a TV show with black men taking on the mockery of their own people. (There were protests and eventually the shows ended but not before working their way into popular culture, repeating negative stereotypes of black people.) At the same time, the Tarzan films were big at the movie theaters and in reruns on TV. Here was this heroic white man—a big, strong, civilized white man—

swinging through the jungle on vines, swooping into villages to "tame" the natives, the African natives. The message of those shows and others was clear: black people can't take care of themselves; they need white people to show them the way. Those messages were in the air we breathed, impossible to ignore and impossible not to internalize. That was bullying, too, cultural bullying, berating, beating, mentally and emotionally and sometimes physically.

A lot of people today who are bullied—black, white, Hispanic, Asian, LGBTQ, whoever, wherever—can relate. Now, like then, the answer is always education, education, education. It's the only thing, the one and only thing that works. Does it work by itself? No. It is not magical. But it is powerfully transformational. We have to enact laws and policies, and fight injustice. We have to mobilize, advocate, and reform. And it takes education as a first step to enable those changes to even begin. It is the means or path to all change.

I KNEW THAT somehow, from my parents, from my siblings, from that sixth-grade teacher. I had my own mantra (I didn't know to call it that back then), which was "Education is the key to success." I wrote it down, I put it on the door to my room, inside my schoolbooks, if I got an A on a paper, everywhere. I don't know where I got it but I must have said it a thousand times in my own head, day in and day out. It was my obsession. I wanted to be a good kid, I wanted to be strong, I wanted to escape poverty, I wanted to get ahead (where, I didn't know yet), I wanted my parents to be proud of me, I wanted to see more and be more. And I had to fight all those barriers to get there. And by the grace of God, and by my parents' home and religion, and some guidance, and some luck, and never using drugs, and my own intuition, whatever was within me, I got to where I am today. It was education, in one form or another, that got me here. Education is the key to success.

I remember once when I was in middle school, we had a counselor who would call students in and ask you how things were going and what you wanted to be when you had finished school. I admired lawyers, from what I'd seen or read or heard about them, and what I recalled from one indelible experience that I tell later in this book, and what I pictured lawyers to be—smart leaders who helped other people get through life. So I told this counselor I wanted to be a lawyer. The counselor just looked at me and smiled politely, like you do with someone who is naïve and doesn't understand the "real world" and he said, "Why don't you aim a little lower? Maybe you should be a teacher." I was discouraged, deflated, like the air had been knocked out of me. (I didn't realize until much later that not only was he saying I wasn't good enough or smart enough to be a lawyer but he was also saying that being a teacher was a second-class career.) I went home and told my mother the story. My mother was furious. She told me, "Don't you ever let someone else tell you what you can be. Never." I will never forget the fury in her eyes and her voice. That never left me. That probably made me more determined to be a lawyer than anything else that ever happened to me. And I've passed that message on to many people, and to every graduating class I've ever addressed at a commencement ceremony, and there have been more than I can count. Education is the key to success, not what some person tells you that you can or cannot be. The postscript is that the middle school counselor came to me as one of my early law clients.

That was my fuel for the next few years. I went to City College High School in Baltimore, which was highly competitive, all boys, black and white, one of the best schools in the state or the country at the time. I had to take a bus, actually several buses, to get there, all the way across town from where I lived, probably eight or nine miles and literally hours, but it was okay because it was my ticket to college and to becoming a lawyer. I had to do it. The way I saw it, I didn't have a choice. I just had to. My father would say there's no such word as "can't" in your vocabulary. I couldn't say, I can't do it. I couldn't even think it. I had come a long way from special ed and I was breathing the fresh air of real education. There are so many comparisons I could make: flying like a bird and nothing was going to ground me. Or like a mechanic who's trying to fix a car and then, aha, you figure it out! Or a math problem on the blackboard and you go through all the steps and you're stuck but then boom, there's the answer. I'm not bragging but I didn't just do *well* in high school, I *thrived*. I was the president of the senior class. I graduated near the very top of my class.

I went on to Howard University in Washington, D.C., and I just kept at it, saying and living my mantra—education is the key to success—becoming president of my sophomore class and earning my Phi Beta Kappa key. Man, I never thought a little kid from South Baltimore from sharecropper parents could do that but my parents thought so, and they were right. Don't let anybody tell you what you can or cannot do. There's no such word as "can't."

I went on to law school at the University of Maryland. I was one driven student. When everybody went on weekend breaks or vacations, I studied. I had my own regime starting on Friday night. I'd get some Chinese food, a carton or two, and I'd go to the library at about six thirty and from then until midnight I'd study, reading cases, rereading, doing the questions, looking up answers, and then head home to get some sleep. The next day I'd do my wash and get ready for the next week. Then I'd go to the library from two in the afternoon until six and then see my girlfriend at night, maybe go to a movie or have dinner. On Sunday I'd go to church and unwind, but just a little, then back to the library until seven or eight at night. (Libraries had been my second home since those days of special ed.) Most of the students wouldn't do as much as I did. They'd study enough to get by but I was a man with no alternative; this is what I was here to do, my destiny, no distractions, nothing to throw me off course. And nothing did.

In those days there were quotas for how many black people could go to law school and how many would be allowed to pass the bar. I did both. And I passed the bar on the first time, which was very uncommon for African-American students.

After law school, I set up private practice, doing criminal defense and small commercial work. Because of what I'd seen in the quota system, I started my own course to tutor young African-American law graduates—to prepare them for the Maryland state bar exam. With a small staff of black and white attorneys, we tutored young lawyers-to-be to give them a better shot at passing the exam, and we improved the outcome dramatically. I didn't do it for money or notoriety or publicity. I did it because without it, the odds were tilted against black students. It was unfair and I set out to make it more fair.

What I didn't know was that some people were aware of it, in particular Lena King Lee, a teacher and attorney herself (only the third black woman to earn a law degree from the University of Maryland), who was serving in the Maryland General Assembly and had founded the Legislative Black Caucus. She hadn't even entered politics until age sixty and after many years of serving was leaving her seat. She called me to meet and talk. She told me she was going to retire and had been looking for a female black attorney to take her place but hadn't found the right person. Then she heard about my free bar exam course, researched me, and decided I should succeed her in the General Assembly. As she put it, "you'll do," high praise from a woman of high standards. She promised me her fund-raising, her support, and her help getting my campaign off the ground, without which I wouldn't have a chance. I'd had exactly zero ambitions of going into politics until that moment. But she persuaded me that public service was my calling, our calling, and it must be done.

That was yet another turning point in my life—knowing which voice to listen to. For the next fourteen years, I served in the Maryland House of Delegates, all the while keeping most of my law practice going (state legislators don't make much money), and like Lena I became chairman of the Legislative Black Caucus. Later I was the first African-American voted speaker pro tem, the number two role in the House. And as far as I was concerned that would be my entire political career. If events hadn't intervened again.

Driving home from the state capital, Annapolis, one day late in 1995, I heard on the radio that a member of the U.S. House, Kweisi Mfume, was leaving his position representing the 7th Congressional District to become the head of the NAACP, throwing his seat open. I wouldn't have challenged Kweisi in a million years and I sure wasn't waiting for him to retire since he was only a couple years my senior. And I wasn't looking toward national office. But some folks started talking to me, urging me, convincing me, and pretty soon I figured it's better to try, even if I fail, than to not try at all. I could still hear Lena Lee telling me to serve the best way I could. It was a seven-way primary race that eventually narrowed down, and I emerged as the Democratic candidate. Then I won in a special election against the Republican with more than 80 percent of the vote. I won again in the regular election in November.

In 1996, in Washington, D.C., I began my first term as a member of the United States House of Representatives. My mother and father were there with me. My sharecropper, modestly educated, working two jobs, raising seven kids, weekend preacher parents lived to see me rise from South Baltimore to the halls of Congress. In the shadow of the Capitol, under the U.S. Constitution, I took the oath of office. That day, I saw my father weeping, openly, trying to wipe away his tears. I don't think I could remember ever seeing my father cry. I asked him about it. "Daddy, were you crying?" I think I secretly wanted him to lie, to say, "No, no, I was perspiring." But he said, "Yes. Yes, I'm crying." Why? I asked him. Because your son is now in the U.S. Congress? He said, "This is great. This is a great moment. Do not get me wrong but I kept looking at your hand. I realized that the same blood that runs in your hand runs in mine." I nodded. He said, "Elijah, isn't this the place where they used to call us slaves?" "Yessir," I answered him. "Isn't this the place they called us three-fifths of a man?" "Yessir," I answered him. "Isn't this the place they called us chattel?" "Yessir." I'll never forget what he said next. "When I see you sworn in today, now I see what I could have been if I had an opportunity."

He and my mother gave me that opportunity. The bond of family is unbreakable. When things go well. And even more so in times that test us.

Family is unbreakable. Yet, if I have one regret over my lifetime, it's that my family life has been imperfect. I'd been raised to believe in the unbreakability of family and that's what I carried into my first marriage so many years ago. We were married young, very young, but we had a beautiful daughter, Jennifer, who is now grown and has followed me into the political arena as a consultant, today the senior director of communications at the Business Roundtable. I've taken her to Congress, to the White House, to meet presidents. Nothing makes me prouder than to say that Jennifer Cummings is my daughter. But the honest truth is, my marriage to her mother did not work. I can't say it was my wife's fault. Or mine. I can only say it was not meant to be. But how could that be? That didn't fit the model I was raised with—the unbreakable family—or my religion and the word of the Bible. That's why it took me a long, long time to finally face that reality. I had to reconcile that sometimes two people—two good people—are not meant to live under the same roof. Later I had another daughter, Adia, aspiring artist, photographer, videographer. Both of my daughters followed my lead/prodding by going to Howard University. Both have made me so proud. Each came from a different time and place in my life. Each is bonded to me forever.

So are my brothers and sisters. But as I confided in Maya on many occasions, I have sometimes put caring for my larger family—neighbors, constituents, people of Baltimore—ahead of my own family. My siblings, even as adults, have a tradition of monthly dinners, on the second Sunday of the month. When I met Maya, I hadn't attended much. I knew they loved me and admired the work I did—my calling—but we had all just grown apart. Well, they hadn't but I had. Maya encouraged me to change that, to reconnect with my siblings, to restore the bonds that had been so strong when I was growing up. We began to attend and it was wonderful for everyone. Reminiscent, warm, funny. Maya learned a lot at those gatherings. Like all of our nicknames. I wasn't called Elijah inside the Cummings family. Early on, my brother James nicknamed me Bobby . . . which made no sense since we had another brother named Robert . . . but it all made sense to us and we laughed and relived stories that only we knew and shared.

Those suppers ended up being some of the most important moments in my life, and I hope in Maya's. She told me she had grown up with traditions like that and knew how important they were. She even urged me to share hosting of family holidays at our house—Thanksgiving and Christmas. I treasure those times—they're the source of sustenance for me.

When my mother had a stroke at the age of eighty-nine, she was frail and failing, but she did not spend one moment, not a single moment, for the next two years without one of us by her side. For two solid years there was a family member in the room with her. We didn't discuss it or plan it; we just did it. We were there until the day she left us. As family.

What I learned over a lifetime—and it has taken a lifetime—is that family may change, but the principles of family remain unbreakable. In God's eyes, the right thing to do is to be true to yourself.

AS STRONG AS our family has been, that strength has not made us immune to tragedy. Our family, like so many, had their own story of a young black man lost to the cliché of urban violence. Our Freddie Gray. Long after I had gone on to Congress, my nephew Christopher died, or rather was murdered. Christopher was the son of my brother James, and his wife, Rosa, two wonderful people and parents. They lived in northern Virginia, in what I joked was a black version of a *Leave It to Beaver* life, a happy, safe, close family with lots of love. No surprise, Christopher was one of those magical, charismatic kids who steal your heart. He was such a good kid; he started his own lawn care business at age thirteen, was very close to his father, and had always been a favorite of mine. I knew I was a role model for him, he told me. I invited him to a picnic at the White House and he met Michelle Obama and had his picture taken with her. Man, was he thrilled. He got more and more interested in politics. At family gatherings, he'd pull me aside and say, "Uncle Eli"— that's what he called me—"tell me about your work." He was fascinated with what I did in Congress, with my life, and how I got to where I was. Christopher wrote a term paper about his heroes, Barack Obama and me. That's some high compliment.

When it was time for him to go off to college, I tried to convince him to go to Howard for undergraduate school like I did, told him what a good education I'd gotten, about the value of attending one of the HBCUs—historically black colleges and universities—and how it impacted my whole life in terms of knowledge and heritage. I talked to him about why I chose to go to the University of Maryland for law school, that my father said I should go there because his tax dollars paid for it and it was "our school." But he didn't want an HBCU or a state school. He wanted to be where a lot of his friends were going, Old Dominion University in Norfolk, Virginia. Academically, he did very well in college, but evidently—and we never got real proof of this—he got involved with some bad folks, with some neighbors, not all college kids, during his junior year. There was some talk later that he was selling marijuana as a little business, following his entrepreneurial nature but not in a wise way.

One day I got a call from his mother, distraught, crying, telling me I had to help her reach his father, James. Christopher and another boy had been shot around four o'clock in the morning, had been taken to the hospital—this was now about ten in the morning—and James was on his way to the hospital. His wife was trying to get to him to tell him instead to go to the police station. When she said that, it sent a chill through me. I knew what it meant. Christopher had died. There was no longer anything to do at the hospital; it was over. The rest would be handled by the authorities.

I walked out of my meeting and sat down to make the hardest phone call of my life. I reached James and told him to pull his car to the side of the road. My brother doesn't show much emotion but I knew he'd fall apart. Losing a child—nothing can prepare you for that, nothing. The birth of a child takes your breath away. The death of a child takes your heart. Now my brother would have to identify his own son's body, then he would have to go to the house where the boys lived near the campus to verify the address; he'd have to tend to the details of tragedy. I still remember when later, we all went to the apartment to lay flowers down and you could see dried blood and gray matter, brains, still on the walls, in the crime scene. That image will never leave my mind. What a loss of life, of what could have been.

I was asked to deliver the eulogy at the funeral. I'd been to hundreds of funerals of young men, mostly black men, who'd been shot down. Now this was one of our own family members. I talked about what Christopher had hoped to be and do, none of which would ever happen. His dreams had been snuffed out. He wouldn't follow in the steps of his uncle Eli, or President Obama, or make his own, unique footsteps. It made me appreciate my own journey, to reach the place I am in life. It broke my heart to see that just taken away, gone, not to be. Whatever Christopher thought of the day before would never emerge the next day. All that was there in the church was a body, a shell that looked like a man/boy that used to be there. His family had sent him off to college, to get a degree and see what life held. He came back to us in a coffin.

What happened to Christopher? We don't know. We will probably never know. The police said maybe it was a botched robbery; maybe a guy was coming to square a crossed deal with Christopher; maybe Christopher got himself involved in bad stuff and thought he could smile and charm his way out because it always seemed to work for him. His parents did everything right but something still went wrong. Parents blame themselves even when there is no blame. Parents and kids are like a bow and arrow. You pull back, and back, as you raise them, trying to aim so straight, trying to put them on a good line, with love and affection, and finally you have to let go. And hope.

Every day is unsure. For all of us. I tell my young staffers, please be careful on your way home from work, or at that community meeting, or this weekend when you're out with your friends. There are good people hurt and killed by bad people every day. I still remember back when I was at Howard University in 1971, and it was in a pretty tough neighborhood (today it's much more gentrified). At orientation they'd tell the students, "Look out for the block," which meant the "block boys," what I knew well from when I was growing up, but a lot of other students didn't know. One night my roommates and I were watching television, a football game I think, and one of these block boys came in and told us to lie down on the floor and not move or he'd kill us. He took the TV and some money from our wallets, but I knew enough to get everyone to lie down and be still. If you grow up with it, you know you're not going to win that one.

My nephew was a brilliant young man, but I don't think he was so wise, street-wise. I'd have told him that if a guy comes in to rob you, put your hands up and say, "Take it." You're not getting out of that one with a smile or charm. Get out with your life. I learned a lot about that from practicing law. Sometimes I represented guys who had robbed and shot someone. I'd once asked a client why he shot the other guy and he said, "Mr. Cummings,

he shouldn't have resisted. When he moved, I had to shoot him."
Had to shoot him—that's a mentality you cannot fight.

To this day, Christopher's murder isn't solved. Solving it won't bring him back but allowing it to go unsolved is a glaring injustice. It's another of thousands of crimes by or on black people that are left without answers. It's as if, because the victim is black, and maybe the perpetrator is, too, it's okay to let it go. *It's what they did to each other.* How is that any different than what the doctor said about my grandfather when he was dying? *He's only a nigger.* No, that is not justice. That keeps injustice going. It's racial and it's racist, no two ways about it.

What came of Christopher's death? Again, pain. So much pain. We must somehow stop this violence, to have real gun laws, to educate, and to reset the norms so that on any block in Baltimore, or St. Louis, or Los Angeles, you can't get a gun as easily as you get a pack of cigarettes, so there will not be so many funerals of young people, black and white. So there will not be so many Christophers. Once again, the pain becomes passion and the passion fuels the purpose. We must change the outcomes of injustice—on the streets, at the ballot box, in schools, in Congress.

I remind myself of that every day that I go to work. Yet another impetus to hurry. Hurry to right wrongs. Hurry to end unjust deaths. Hurry to find alternatives to violence. Hurry to give young black men hope instead of despair. Hurry to change fate. Hurry, Elijah, hurry.

CHAPTER 3

Our
Turn

The 2018 midterm election was historic. It may well be
a turning point in history, the moment that saved our
democracy. But that depends on what we do with the
moment.

When Trump was elected in 2016, the Republicans carried
the presidency, the Senate, and the House. That virtually shut
down any transparency in government, any bipartisan compro-
mise, any respect for constitutional and institutional checks and
balances, any resistance to the whim of the president. It was
Trump's government to run in whatever way he wanted. We
have had all of those branches of the government controlled by
one side before but never have we had such planned obstruction
and blatant scorn of the other side. This wasn't just a one-party
majority; it was the other party be damned.

In the first two years of his presidency, from January 2017 to November 2018, the Trump administration (aided by an obedient Republican Senate and House) compiled an unprecedented litany of accomplishments ranging from dubious to unconstitutional: His presidential campaign was suspected to be the target of, and possible willing partner in, Russian interference. He is accused of making an estimated 15,000-plus false or misleading statements—also known as lies; he turned his Twitter thumbs into weapons of name-calling, threatening, and bullying; he called any reporting that was critical "fake news"; he even banned the *New York Times*, CNN, the BBC, and other media from press briefings, and he gave a not-too-subtle bow to white supremacists in Charlottesville. He rolled back environmental protections, pulled out of the Paris Climate Agreement, and called man-made climate change a hoax. He tried repeatedly to repeal the Affordable Care Act/Obamacare, did his best to dismantle it piece by piece, and tried to cut spending on Medicare, Medicaid, and Social Security Disability Insurance. He pushed the Supreme Court further to the right by ramming through two appointments, one of whom was accused of sexual assault. He repealed key portions of Dodd-Frank's post-2008 constraints on banks, pulled out of the Trans-Pacific Partnership, enacted punitive tariffs on steel and other imports, and cut taxes for the rich—corporate and estate taxes. He met with strongman Kim Jong-Un of North Korea, flirted with and flattered Russian despot Vladimir Putin, and withdrew from the Iran nuclear arms deal. He issued his Muslim ban, despite constant rejection by the courts; demanded funding for his border wall, despite resistance from all quarters, resulting in a government shutdown; ended the Dreamers Act (to protect immigrant children); and imposed a cruel family separation policy at the southern border. He fired FBI director James Comey, it seems for a variety of reasons, including refusing to drop his investigation of Michael Flynn and focusing on the Russian election interference; he faced a special counsel investigation by Robert Mueller into that Russian interference and alleged collusion related to the 2016 election, and saw multiple advisors convicted of criminal charges. All this in less than twenty-four months. It was record-setting . . . in a bad way, a very bad way.

But fortunately we still have elections (despite the brazen efforts at voter suppression and calculated gerrymandering). The voter turnout in the midterms, typically low as elections go, was record-setting for 2018, the highest in over a hundred years. In fact, turnout in nonpresidential years had been going steadily down, until now. The last time we had a strong showing at the polls was at the height of the Vietnam War and protests, when millions of people were angered by the government's commitment to the war—the draft and deaths of our children in a battle between two sides most of us didn't understand, a battle we couldn't win. People were mad and they showed it at the polls. Sound familiar?

Ironically, we can thank President Trump for the record voter turnout in 2018. It was largely a reaction and backlash to the way he and his partisan Congress had governed for his first two years.

The Democrats gained 41 seats in the House, lost 2 seats in the Senate, but picked up 7 governorships, over 350 state legislative seats, and majorities in 6 more statehouses. Thankfully, after so many consecutive terms, my seat was not in jeopardy. Last election, my constituents reelected me with more than 75 percent of the vote, so instead of campaigning for myself, I set out to help every Democrat I possibly could. I used my reputation to raise money for candidates who weren't as well known but whom we desperately needed—in swing districts, inner cities, rural farmlands, anywhere we could win a seat.

This was such an intense, fateful, anxious, angry, hopeful, emotionally charged moment that on election night, late-night talk show hosts—Jimmy Fallon, Jimmy Kimmel, Stephen Colbert—made it the topic of their opening monologues. To convince his liberal audience that he wasn't just delivering an optimistic spin on the results, Colbert put the live feed of conservative, Trump-loving Fox News on his studio monitors as their anchors called the House in favor of the Democrats. It was an undeniable blue wave; even Fox said so!

It was a year of minorities, of color, of gays, of an openly bisexual U.S. senator, but more than anything, it was the year of women. The total in the House is now 102 (89 Democrats, 13 Republicans), with 31 of those females being first-timers, including the first Democratic Latina governor, two Native Americans, one of whom is the first LGBTQ member of Congress, the first two Muslim women in Congress, the first black woman elected from Massachusetts, and the youngest woman ever elected to Congress, at twenty-nine years old. Democratic candidates homed in like lasers on the issues, including repeal of parts of the Affordable Care Act, health care overall, Russian interference in the 2016 election, income inequality and tax cuts for the wealthy, immigration cruelty, and racial division—the issues that energized and motivated voters, the Vietnam War of 2018. It was a "blue wave" for sure, but it was a blue wave of women!

It's no surprise that in spite of some rumblings for change, Nancy Pelosi, one of the savviest politicians in history, after serving as minority leader from 2011 to 2019, was elected Speaker of the House, the role she had for four years under George W. Bush. I cannot say enough about Nancy Pelosi. We are close, not only politically but personally (her roots are also in Baltimore, the daughter and sister of two Baltimore mayors). My respect knows no limits. She is steady—a rock in a storm. There are so few like her in Washington. Nancy could ask me to walk across hot coals and I would say, what time and where? She has a built-in barometer for the mechanics and emotions of lawmaking. I often turn to her for wisdom. Over the years, it has become a two-way street. There is no higher compliment than for Nancy Pelosi to ask, "Elijah, what do you think we should do?"

One of Speaker Pelosi's first decisions in 2018 was asking me to head the House Committee on Oversight and Reform. The job of the Oversight Committee is wide in scope, and among the most powerful in government: "The Committee on Oversight and Reform is the main investigative committee in the U.S. House of Representatives. It has the authority to investigate the subjects within the Committee's legislative jurisdiction as well as 'any matter' within the jurisdiction of the other standing House Committees." There are some potent words in there: "*main investigative committee*" with jurisdiction on "*any matter . . .*" In effect, the committee acts as the conscience of the government. That includes federal civil service, status of officers and employees of the United States, their compensation, classification, and retirement; government management and accounting measures; overall economy, efficiency, and management of government operations, federal procurement, population, and demography, including the census, postal service, public information and records, relationship of the federal government to the states, and reorganization of the executive branch of the government. The chairman is one of only three with the power to issue subpoenas even without a committee vote.

When the Speaker asked me to serve, I was proud to accept. She stood by my side as I put my hand on the Bible, held by Maya, and took the oath of office as chair. (Yes, I thought about my father weeping at my first swearing in. He might well have been weeping again.) It was the second time Nancy Pelosi had asked me to serve on the Oversight Committee, the first time when she was minority leader during the Republican majority of Obama's second term, at which time I became the ranking member under GOP chairs Darrell Issa, Jason Chaffetz, and Trey Gowdy. Fatefully, as it turned out, she also asked me to be on Gowdy's subcommittee—the select committee to investigate the Benghazi incident.

IF YOU CONDUCT yourself with a conscience, you take the mandate of a congressional committee as a responsibility and not a weapon; you don't use it as a political baseball bat. Supposedly, and I emphasize supposedly, that select committee was to look into the 2012 terrorist attack on our government offices in Benghazi, Libya, and the deaths of our ambassador to Libya, Christopher Stevens, and three other Americans. The stated purpose of the investigation (which stretched from 2014 to the end of 2016, at a cost of $7 million) was to determine exactly what had happened, why, and what could have been done to prevent it. Instead—and there's no two ways about it—Benghazi was a witch hunt, a prolonged, exaggerated, politically motivated, scapegoating attempt to use a tragic event to destroy one person, Hillary Clinton.

From minute one, it became clear, the purpose was to blame then–secretary of state Clinton, particularly after she became the Democratic presidential nominee. The investigation put her under constant scrutiny, accusation, and presumed guilt—at one point including an eleven-hour grilling of Secretary Clinton herself. The final eight-hundred-page report showed tragic errors in protecting the diplomats by the State Department, the CIA (underestimation of danger after overthrow of Khaddafi), and the Defense Department (failure to rescue the Americans), but the report showed absolutely no wrongdoing on Secretary Clinton's part. None.

It did, however, discover that she had used a private email server in addition to her government server, which proved to be a vulnerable point in her presidential campaign, which the FBI kept probing almost until election day. Throughout the investigation, Chairman Gowdy insisted the goal was not to defame Hillary Clinton, but there is no question their work drove her poll numbers lower and gave ammunition to critics throughout the 2016 campaign. The report cleared her but the intended damage was done. I was outraged and I let it be known in my closing statement. I quoted committee chairman Gowdy's own words, complaining that carrying out this investigation was "an impossible job" given the "political environment."

I seized on the hypocrisy of his words. The political environment he condemned was his own party's doing. I said so: "it has been done by his own Republican colleagues in the House on this very issue—Benghazi." I reconstructed how this whole partisan, manufactured so-called investigation began. Two years of hearings were conducted by the Republican-run House Intelligence Committee, Senate Intelligence Committee, and House Homeland Security Committee—two full years—but Speaker John Boehner didn't like the answers he got. Especially because Secretary Clinton was running for president. Would he have pursued so hard, so incessantly, and so nastily if she were returning to private life? No, this was a bald-faced takedown, not an investigation. Boehner set up a new Select Committee "with no rules, no deadline, and an unlimited budget"—and he set it loose on Hillary Clinton, candidate for president. He and his party were using taxpayer dollars to pay for a political maneuver—thwart the strongest candidate's chances for election. Am I being partisan in saying that? I ask good sense to judge. I ask history to judge. I ask the very words of the Republicans conducting the process to speak for themselves.

Representative Kevin McCarthy—Speaker Boehner's second in command and the chairman's close friend—essentially admitted that they established the select committee to drive down Secretary Clinton's poll numbers. Republican congressman Richard Hanna said the select committee was "designed" to go after Secretary Clinton. That's his word—designed—not mine. One of the chairman's own investigators—a conservative Republican—charged that he was fired in part for not going along with these plans to "hyper focus" on Hillary Clinton. He wasn't partisan enough!

With Secretary Clinton testifying, sitting in front of all of us for the umpteenth hour, I went full bore at the blatant duplicity and disingenuousness of the investigation. "When Speaker Boehner established this Select Committee, he justified it by arguing that it would be 'cross-jurisdictional.' I assumed he meant we would focus on more than just Secretary Clinton and the State Department. But Madam Secretary, you are sitting here by yourself. The Secretary of Defense is not on your left, and the Director of the CIA is not on your right." If that isn't duplicitous, what is? He set out guidelines and threw them out the window . . . for fear the committee might learn something that would hurt their takedown.

I did not stop. I replayed the ugliest personal attacks on Hillary Clinton. Carly Fiorina said Secretary Clinton "has blood on her hands," Mike Huckabee accused her of "ignoring the warning calls from dying Americans in Benghazi," Rand Paul said "Benghazi was a 3:00 a.m. phone call that she never picked up," and Lindsey Graham tweeted, "Where the hell were you on the night of the Benghazi attack?"

Like a good lawyer, I summarized. "[N]one of the 54 witnesses the Committee interviewed substantiated these wild Republican claims. Secretary Clinton did not order the military to stand down. . . . Here is the bottom line. The Select Committee has spent 17 months and . . . million(s) in taxpayer funds. . . . these documents and interviews do not show any nefarious activity. In fact, it's just the opposite. The new information we have obtained confirms and corroborates the core facts we already knew from the eight previous investigations. It is time . . . to start focusing on what we here in Congress can do to improve the safety and security of our diplomatic corps in the future."

The committee had asked their questions, made their accusations, and gotten answers, over and over, from experts, eyewitnesses, career public servants. They just didn't like what they heard. In the words of Colonel Jessup (Jack Nicholson) in the movie *A Few Good Men*, they couldn't "handle the truth."

Years later, as I took the reins of the Oversight Committee, that experience, the partisan behavior, and the outcome were never far from my mind. I knew there would be turnabout, though I didn't know when, or how, or what we would face. I knew it because of my experiences in Congress. And I knew it because of my mother.

HERE I WAS, enlisted in a virtual war with the president of the United States, a crusade for the survival of democracy, a battle of the utmost importance. But in the midst of this national, front-page showdown, in combat with perhaps the world's largest ego, I could lean on what I learned from my mother long ago. She had taught me to "respect the storm" when I was only eight years old. It was an icy morning in Baltimore when my brothers and sisters and I went off to school, so icy we had to be careful not to fall. What we didn't know was that one of our friends in our neighborhood had been crossing the street when a car came by driving too fast. The driver put on the brakes but hit the ice and couldn't stop. The car struck our friend and killed him.

The storm took that little boy's life. We had no idea. We were at school. By the time we walked home, the sun had come out, it was warm, and there was no ice. The storm had passed. But it left behind its damage. "Respect the storm," my mother said. What does it mean? It means when you see the storm, do not act foolishly. Act wisely. Don't throw away your sense. Recognize the power and force of the storm you're in. Think about where you want to be, and who you want to be, when the storm is over. Because all storms, no matter how brutal, eventually pass. We are weathering the storm of a president threatening our values and our heritage. How should we react? Where do we want to be? Who do we want to be? What do we do when the storm relents, even for a moment or a year or two? We must be ready. I use her lesson to govern my actions.

Finally, it was our turn. I vowed to do the job the way I thought it should be done—fairly. And fast. There was so much to do, the challenge was knowing where to start. As I said at the time, "we've gotta hit the ground, not running, but flying."

My staff and I looked at the issues in front of us and set out to prioritize them. We were anxious to get started but wanted to do it right. The president said the new Democratic majority in the House could either help him pass legislation or we could investigate him, but we couldn't do both. I disagreed. And I was determined to show it. We could pass good laws, not just his laws. And we could make sure the government was transparent, open, and honest. Where it wasn't, it would be held accountable.

From the first day, we put in long hours, poring over papers and records, comparing notes and agendas with the other committees, planning where to focus first, which witnesses to call, what documents we would request, where to expect resistance, what the other side's tactics would be, where we could have the greatest impact the soonest—to be effective and efficient. I worked some days in my Baltimore office, but mostly in my office in the Rayburn Building, on the Hill. Every day that I was in Washington, I went back to Baltimore, to my home each night, making calls from the car, working more, planning more, but as often as I could sleeping in my bed in my real house—not far from the neighborhood where I grew up—to stay grounded, to be reminded of where I come from and who I represent. Sometimes on those drives home, I'd wonder where Donald Trump goes to be grounded. Mar-a-Lago? Trump Tower? I'm not saying I'm against luxury or living nicely. Not too long ago I had a fire in my home in Baltimore—I have a tenant, and some form of negligence led to the fire—so I had to move out during the rehab work. Insurance paid for me to live very well, at the Ritz-Carlton residences overlooking the inner harbor of Baltimore. Valet parking, concierge service, mail pickup, umbrellas when it's raining, views of the water, "yes, Mr. Cummings," "of course, Mr. Cummings." While I was there, I realized that if I wanted to, I could move there permanently instead of going back to my house. But that's not who I am. That's not where I come from. I need to be around my roots. Maybe Donald Trump does, too. His roots and mine are very different.

But as modest as my beginnings may have been, I realized that now, at this moment, I had a job to do, maybe the most important work of my life. I was honored, really honored to be able to do this work. And it was so important, not just for us, for now, but for our children, for our future, a future we will never see. So much to do, so fast. Again I thought about what I'd said on day one, "hit the ground, not running, but flying." And that made me think of my father.

"FLYING"—THAT CAME FROM my father. When we were little kids, some weekends he'd say to us, "Clean up, put on your nice clothes, and get in the car. We're going for a ride."

He'd take the whole family to Friendship Airport (what they used to call BWI–Thurgood Marshall Airport), to an area where anyone could watch the planes take off and land. He'd point to a plane that was taxiing on the runway and say, "Where do you think that one is going?" Or he'd see one coming in for a landing and say, "Guess where that one is coming from."

We'd make up stories about the passengers going to visit family, or friends, or off to do business. Going to New York or Miami or Los Angeles or Paris. Anywhere they wanted to go. Anywhere we could think of. It was exciting for us just seeing those big birds soaring into the clouds, going as far as your mind could take you. And nobody liked it better than my father. He told us he and my mom would never fly. They didn't have the money or even places to go. But he'd say to us kids, "You will, you'll fly. Someday. Mark my words. You'll be flying."

Then we'd look up at the sky again and imagine where we'd be going. New places to do new things. Back then, I would imagine it, very literally, a trip. Yes, someday I'd get on a jet, strap on my seat belt, sit back, and go off to another city or country. Later, I realized what he really meant. He was telling us we could *do* whatever we wanted. We could fly, take off, have no limits, change the world. That was flying. Not tied to the ground, not held back. Flying.

When I took on the Oversight Committee, I was flying. In fact, I was the pilot. My father was right.

We had two years to do our work, maybe more if we maintained our majority, but we couldn't count on that. And in reality, there are a lot less than a year's worth of workdays in a congressional year. Congress is only in session a limited number of days, with recesses, holidays, and other interruptions. Oversight had been neglected, or rather avoided or ignored for two full years. With no oversight, there was no reform. The Republican majority didn't want to take a hard look at what was going on, or the way it was being done, and they sure didn't want to fix it. It was like the three monkeys—hear no evil, see no evil, speak no evil. Just pretend everything is okay. Just worry about keeping your seat in Congress.

Now we had to do the stated job of the committee—Oversight *and* Reform. We had to do the former—oversee, look carefully, study, uncover—before we could do the latter—repair, restore, even resuscitate our damaged democracy.

In the time we had, we set out to take on not as many issues as we could, but the most urgent issues that we could take on well—as always, to be effective and efficient.

To me there were two tracks: 1) the Trump presidency—use and abuse of power, and 2) defending our democracy—voting rights, opioid crisis, health care, drug prices, immigration, children's welfare. Where and when the two tracks intersected, and it was too often, those issues rose to the top of our agenda.

Ultimately we held hearings on: prescription drug pricing

(despite direct communications from Republican leadership to the pharma companies warning them not to comply with the investigation); Michael Cohen, Trump's former personal lawyer; the administration's opioid policy; transparency, or a lack of it; the Freedom of Information Act; EPA and Department of the Interior practices, and Department of Justice positions; the census issue (and attempts to add a discriminatory citizenship question); failure to comply with subpoenas by the Departments of Justice, Homeland Security, and Health and Human Services; violations of the Hatch Act (Kellyanne Conway refusing to testify); failure of government departments to supply legally requested documents—FBI, GSA, and others; attempts to dismantle the Affordable Care Act; immigration—border treatment of children and families by ICE and the child separation policy; the Mueller testimony; environmental policy; and potential violations of the emoluments clause—improper income and profit to government figures while in office (benefiting Trump-owned properties). And we had to do it all in a handful of actual days that Congress is in session.

We knew that at every turn the Trump White House, in their total disdain and disrespect for the Constitution and the balance of power the founding fathers established, would do everything in their power to block us. Trump had been promising to "build a wall" since his campaign. Ironically, he was building a wall of obstruction around Congress to stop us from doing our job. Our challenge was to get around, over, and through the wall. When I face problems like that, I turn to geometry. Literally.

When I was in the tenth grade at Baltimore City College High School, we were required to take geometry. At that point in my life, it was probably the most challenging course I had ever taken. Each night, the instructor would give us at least ten, sometimes more, very difficult problems to solve for homework. There were times when I would spend literally hours on one problem. Sometimes eventually, I'd crack it. In some cases, no matter how long I tried, I just could not figure it out. I'd go to school the next morning frustrated, still thinking, still confused. The instructor would then ask one of my classmates who had arrived at the solutions to work out each one on the blackboard. I had labored long and hard, sometimes without any success, but I wasn't discouraged or mad that other students found the answers and I didn't. It was the opposite. I was always excited to see the solutions, to see what steps I missed in my efforts, to see where the answer was hidden.

The second a classmate got to that part of the problem where I'd gotten stuck, I would experience one of those "aha" moments. I literally would feel chills down my spine because now I saw what I was doing wrong. I saw what I missed. Most important, I knew what to do next time. If I had to solve a similar problem in the future, I would have a path to follow, what to do and what not to do. I also realized that if I had not tried so hard to solve the homework assignment, seeing a classmate work the problems out on the blackboard would have meant very little. If I had given up, as lots of students did, I wouldn't have cared about the right answer. It made me think about so many kids who give up on studying and school altogether. Once they do, they may never feel that aha moment. For me, this wasn't just a lesson in geometry; it was a lesson in sticking with a problem until you figure it out, and getting joy, real joy, out of finding an answer. It was what learning is all about.

Why tell this story now, all these years later? It didn't lead me to become a geometry teacher. It didn't even make me very good at geometry. It did much more for me. It gave me a gift—one of my gifts has always been the willingness to work hard, even in the face of discouragement. If ever I fail in my efforts to accomplish a goal—a test, a job, a case, an election, a congressional vote—I always try to figure out what I did wrong, or what I failed to do, or what I didn't persuade a colleague or adversary to do, or what I just missed (like what I saw on the blackboard)—and then to try again and again until I find a way.

I believe every one of us, no matter what we do—doctor, lawyer, public servant, businessperson, fireman, cop, teacher, mother, father, student, friend—should set goals, problems to solve, things to strive for. It may sound a little old-fashioned, but if you don't set a goal, you don't know how you're doing. What's important to me—what I tell other people, especially young people in commencement addresses, in church, at my office, in my neighborhood—is that if we do not immediately reach our goals, and most of the time we won't on the first or second (or third) try, don't call it failure, call it progress. Learn from your mistakes and do it differently the next time. And if that doesn't work, learn again, and do it differently. Again and again.

In our present dilemma/predicament/disaster with the Trump administration and all the challenges and brick walls, it would be easy to give up, to say I can't find a solution. This geometry problem can't be solved. I'm not willing to give up that easily.

I've heard many of my congressional colleagues, both Republicans and Democrats, say that they plan to leave Congress soon, to not even try to run again, because they cannot get anything meaningful done, they can't get through to the White House, or the president himself, to do what needs to be done for their constituents. I understand. I empathize. But I don't agree with throwing in the towel. Sure, I may get frustrated, angry, even outraged over our failure to get meaningful legislation done on opioid abuse, the Affordable Care Act, voting rights, immigration, and infrastructure, you name it. Both sides agree we need to address these and both sides are discouraged. But we must not give up. We must find solutions. We must learn from our mistakes and from each other so that we can be more effective and efficient in the future. The stakes are so very high, and our people deserve nothing less. We have to go back to our homework until we get it right. Geometry. Aha.

CHAPTER 4

The Hearings— and Being Heard

In mid-January of my first year chairing the Oversight Committee, I announced our first investigation and hearing: "The Committee on Oversight and Reform is investigating the actions of drug companies in raising prescription drug prices in the United States, as well as the effects of these actions on federal and state budgets and on American families. For years, drug companies have been aggressively increasing prices on existing drugs and setting higher launch prices for new drugs while recording windfall profits. The goals of this investigation are to determine why drug companies are increasing prices so dramatically, how drug companies are using the proceeds, and what steps can be taken to reduce prescription drug prices."

In my opening statement, I acknowledged the contribution of "big pharma," the leading pharmaceutical companies. "Research and development efforts on groundbreaking medications have made immeasurable contributions to the health of Americans, including new treatments and cures for diseases that have affected people for centuries." But I made it clear that that did not let them off the hook for social responsibility and accountability, saying "the ongoing escalation of prices by drug companies is unsustainable."

It's worth noting what the inaugural investigation of the committee was not. It was not a partisan issue, in any way. It wasn't looking into Trump's finances or immigration policies or obstruction of justice. It was about what for too many people is a life-or-death issue, affording the medicines that keep people alive—all people, Democrats, Republicans, young, old, black, white, brown, gay, straight, LGBTQ. It wasn't left, right, or center. The cost of prescription drugs affects every single person in the country, sick people and families of sick people. Americans pay more for our medicines than any other Western nation. *We pay too much for the privilege to live.* It is not a privilege; it is, or should be, a right. It was the issue I raised to Trump on our first meeting after he took office. I told him that action to lower costs was something he could do for all people, not just his base, something that would benefit everyone. Almost everyone. The pharmaceutical companies are the only group in the United States that opposes more reasonable pricing.

On January 10, 2019, we launched what would amount to the most in-depth investigation to date into big pharma's pricing practices. We sent written requests to twelve leading pharmaceutical companies requesting information on policy and practice, internal and industry communications on price increases, percentages of profits invested in research, and corporate strategies to maintain and grow market share and exercise pricing power.

We had a lot of information about drug costs and drug profits before the investigations began, shocking, sometimes frightening information. Not only is there a brutal burden on individuals, but the government itself is facing a budget-breaking future through Medicare and Medicaid. Medicare Part D is the primary prescription drug insurance for older Americans—43 million people at a cost of $99 billion. That's a big number, but maybe that's just the cost of taking care of so many older people. Maybe the costs are legitimate and just a fact of life. Or maybe not. *The twenty costliest drugs account for over a third of that $99 billion—$37 billion.* Let that sink in. That means if your company makes just one of those medications, you clear over one and a half billion dollars—billion, with a "B"—just from Medicare Part D, not to mention what you might make via other insurance or even uninsured patients. The payments under Part D for branded drugs went up more than 60 percent from 2011 to 2015 (when inflation was barely over 2 percent). More than 90 percent of the popular drugs doubled in price in that same time. In 2018, there were increases in the price of 4,400 drugs and decreases in only 46 drugs. And it is not as if the increases are all covered by Medicare insurance. The number of people on Part D paying

$2,000 or more out of pocket doubled from 2011 to 2015. A survey by the Kaiser Family Foundation showed that 20 percent, or one out of every five people, did not fill a prescription because it cost too much! Think about that when you walk down the street. Count the next five people and realize the fifth one cannot afford his or her medicine.

We knew a lot going in. But we knew there was a lot we didn't know. So we asked the leaders in the industry: Tell us how you run your business. We know you have costs of distribution and sales. We know you have to invest in research. We know you have competition. We know you're in business to make a profit. Just tell us how it works—why you charge what you charge.

No surprise, they didn't want us, or anyone, looking into their practices. But if the Congressional Committee on Oversight and Reform makes a formal request, what could they do?

Especially since it looked like the Trump administration also claimed to have a genuine interest in taking on the challenge of lowering costs. The hearings were scheduled to start on January 29. That morning, Mark Meadows (Republican from North Carolina and member of the Oversight Committee) told me that the president was "serious about working in a bipartisan way to lower prescription drug prices. . . . When I spoke to him last night he wanted to make sure I conveyed that to you." Maybe, just maybe, that conversation I'd had with Trump in his first week as president had stuck with him. Maybe it just took longer to find the right moment. Maybe now was the time. I told Meadows, "We are willing, able, and ready to work with them to get this done and thank you."

On Tuesday, January 29, at 11 a.m., the hearings began. The

purpose had been spelled out: determine why prices were increasing so fast and find ways to lower them. The background information was cited, including the effects on government budgets and on American families, evidence of price increases in the past few years, and the windfall profits. Expert witnesses entered their testimony; industry documents and testimony were to come later. We had the experts of experts: Dr. Gerard Anderson, professor of health policy and management at Johns Hopkins; Dr. Catherine Alicia Georges, national volunteer president of AARP; Dr. Aaron Kesselheim, associate professor at Harvard Medical School; and Avik S. A. Roy, president of the Foundation for Research on Equal Opportunity. They knew policy and how it could or should mesh with commerce; they knew the power of breakthrough medicines; they knew the realities of research and development costs; they knew the onerous weight that health care places on families and institutions. Their facts were indisputable.

But the true impact and tragedy of the crisis came to life through the words of one woman who spoke from experience, Antoinette Worsham, mother of two daughters, both type 1 diabetics. She told us about her older daughter, Antavia, who was diagnosed at the age of sixteen but only lived to twenty-two, solely because of the high cost of insulin. When she was too old to qualify for help from the BCMH (Bureau for Children with Medical Handicaps), she self-rationed. That's a nice way of saying she cut her doses in half or less in the hope she could survive, even weaker and more at risk, by stretching the medicine out. It doesn't work, at least not for long. When type 1 diabetics ration insulin it can cause diabetes ketoacidosis, an increase in toxic ketones that can lead to coma and death. The doctor didn't tell her to ration her insulin. She did it because she had no choice. It was all she could afford. It's like diluting soup until it's nothing but water and no nutrition. Eventually you die. And she did . . . because she couldn't get the drug that could keep her alive. No other reason. I wanted the committee and the country to hear that, and hear it from the mother who lost her. I wanted people to feel what it would be like to lose a child for a reason that could have been prevented. I hoped maybe even the president could feel that.

But Antoinette Worsham wasn't finished. She told us about her younger daughter, Antanique, who was diagnosed with the same disease at the age of twelve, and was now eighteen and a freshman in college. She said to us, "I fear the same thing will happen to Antanique when she turns twenty-one." I wanted everyone in that room to feel that fear. Imagine that you lose a child and then you see a picture of losing yet another child the very same way. A way that is preventable. A way that we could stop with the stroke of a pen.

Even the harshest cynics on the committee were silent and stunned as she went on. She asked, "How [do] pharmaceuticals [companies] think college students are supposed to be able to pay for high drug cost on top of high tuition, room and board? Pharmaceuticals are charging over 5000%. . . . How is allowing pharmaceuticals to price gouge making America great again?" This mother calling out the pharma companies' profiteering from real life—or real death—was more compelling than any testimony from a doctor or nurse or research scientist.

If we weren't doing enough, Antoinette Worsham was trying on her own, one woman, alone. She founded T1Diabetes Journey Inc. in honor of her older daughter, Antavia, to give financial help to diabetics. She said that though the insulin makers claim to have programs to offset costs, it can take two weeks for approval . . . if you qualify. She pleaded, "We need them to fight for affordable health care for all. Not just for those living below or just above poverty."

The government was ignoring the issue. She shamed us. She even laid out the math: A student fresh out of college could make around $40,000 or $3,333 a month. If you subtract $800 for rent, $300 for a car, $170 for insurance, $500 for food, $200 for insurance, another $200 for utilities and phone, $500 to pay back student loans, $150 miscellaneous, and $1,000 for insulin—subtract those expenses and the diabetic comes up almost $500 short. Every month. Six thousand dollars a year. Just to stay alive. She had our attention and she literally begged for our help: "I am crying out and asking for you to review the pharmaceutical drug gouging and make health care affordable for all."

I saw tears in the eyes of my colleagues. I saw sympathy and empathy. I had hope. But we did not see any action. In fact, we saw the opposite. We saw obstruction.

As we prepared for the next step in the hearings and investigations, which was the request for documents and testimony from the drug companies, Republican members of the committee openly urged the companies and their executives *not* to comply with requests from their own committee.

BuzzFeed broke the story:

In an unusual move, House Republicans are warning drug companies against complying with a House investigation into drug prices. Republicans on the House Oversight Committee sent letters to a dozen CEOs of major drug companies warning that information they provide to the committee could be leaked to the public by Democratic chair Elijah Cummings in an effort to tank their stock prices.

The idea that we were doing this to destroy their stock value was nothing but a bizarre conspiracy theory or false narrative. We didn't care if their stock went up, down, or sideways. That was their business. We were there to bring sanity to drug prices. But two of our members, Freedom Caucus leaders Jim Jordan and Mark Meadows, sent their letter to the pharma companies, a blatant scare tactic which would prevent us from helping people afford their medicines. I was outraged and appalled. This wasn't about corporate earnings; it was about keeping people alive. I said loud and clear that these guys would rather "protect drug company stock prices than the interests of the American people." To say what they did was inhumane is an understatement.

Meanwhile the White House, by way of acting chief of staff Mick Mulvaney, moaned on Fox News that they (the administration) "don't get nearly enough attention . . . for what we've done with drug prices." Really? What has the administration done? And who in their ranks wants to do something? The conflicts of interest in the White House and cabinet were, and are, rampant. Health and human services secretary Alex Azar had been CEO of Eli Lilly and while he ran the company they doubled the price of insulin. Is that the guy who is going to help lower drug costs?!

Just like my first meeting with Trump, the hearings were a fleeting hope. It was just lip service from Republicans that must have seemed like the right thing to say at the time. And then was short-lived. The drug companies and their lobbyists did their best to blunt our efforts. Poof, the hope for change was gone, or at least put on a long hold. How do we tell Antoinette Worsham to hold? She's already lost one daughter and may lose another.

We hit a roadblock. But I said this was not the end of the road, just a detour. I could still hear my father telling me the story of his father, the South Carolina preacher who died because two doctors said he was too poor, and maybe too black, to matter, to get the care and medicine that might have saved him. I could see the faces of the folks in my neighborhood, and across the country, who have to decide between food on the table and prescriptions. No, I was not giving up. I was determined to continue the battle for health care, starting with lowering drug costs. This was the start, not the finish. I would just have to use my geometry lessons to find the answer. It might take another formula or theorem but we would keep working on the problem until we found a solution.

Meantime, we had other pressing issues to take on.

"RAISE YOUR RIGHT hand. Do you swear or affirm to tell the whole truth and nothing but the truth?"

The witness affirmed, "I do."

The president's personal lawyer, convicted of campaign finance law violations, tax fraud, bank fraud, and lying to a Senate committee investigating the building of Trump Tower, was addressing the full Oversight Committee. He was willing to tell us exactly how he did what he did on behalf of Donald Trump in business, during the presidential campaign and after.

The chambers were jammed—wall-to-wall media—left, right, and center, with lights, mics, cameras, and smartphones, reporters, pundits, bloggers, and tweeters ready to write, post, stream, and spin, House members and staffers scribbling last-minute notes, whispering tactics and reading lips across the room for clues. Michael Cohen, President Trump's personal attorney and alleged "fixer," was about to testify before the House Committee on Oversight and Reform and the world, live and televised.

Before Cohen could even appear, Trump tried to discredit the testimony in an interview on Fox News by dangling rumors that Cohen is "in trouble on some loans and fraud and taxicabs and stuff that I know nothing about" (but evidently knew enough about to smear Cohen with innuendo). Then Trump added a vague reference to a story about Cohen's father-in-law's money. Trump said Cohen was only testifying to reduce his sentence, ending with his signature comment, "It's pretty sad," Trump's shorthand for "he has turned on me so don't believe him."

I got together with Adam Schiff and Jerry Nadler and we issued a statement warning Trump not to interfere with the hearings: "Our nation's laws prohibit efforts to discourage, intimidate, or otherwise pressure a witness not to provide testimony to Congress." Most presidents would know that, or would listen when their lawyers tell them, but not Donald Trump. Not the intimidator in chief.

I recount and re-create this event here in detail because in the nonstop barrage of Trump offenses, we often forget the one from the day before. Today's crime buries the one from yesterday. We become numb. But we can't. We shouldn't. We must remember. We must stay upset. It reads like a trashy novel. If only it was fiction, but tragically, it is fact.

For the next seven hours Michael Cohen did as he promised. He told the truth, something we had heard very little of the two previous years. Think back to the laundry list of misdeeds already recounted here, accrued over the past 700-plus days, and Michael Cohen addressed some of the most egregious—from the size of the inauguration crowd; to fantasies of voter fraud; to mocking Gold Star war heroes and POWs, including Senator John McCain; to admiring dictators and strongmen Vladimir Putin, Recep Erdogan, and Kim Jong-Un; to defending campaign chairman Paul Manafort in the face of evidence of contact with Russian powers; to dismissing or minimizing intelligence investigations into Russian interference in the 2016 election; to firing FBI director James Comey leading those investigations; to endorsing accused sex predator Roy Moore for the House seat in Alabama; to condoning white nationalists in the Charlottesville march; to threats to fire Attorney General Jeff Sessions, Assistant Attorney General Rod Rosenstein, and Special Counsel Robert Mueller; to disclaiming knowledge of payoffs to porn stars; to invoking executive privilege and dangling presidential pardons for refusing testimony against White House interests; to stonewalling the release of subpoenaed evidence; to undermining freedom of the press by labeling any stories the White House dislikes as "fake news"; to more than nine thousand lies or misstatements as of that date, later topping fifteen thousand, as Kellyanne Conway put it, "alternative facts" from the Trump White House. . . .

After all that, Michael Cohen would spend a full day, the time it takes the president to tell twelve to fifteen lies, detailing the deeds, and answering questions on those deeds, carried out at the behest of Donald J. Trump, candidate and ultimately president of the United States. Michael Cohen told the truth.

My committee, the House Committee on Oversight and Reform, was doing its job—overseeing and, when necessary, reforming. But before we could carry out our duty that day, there were the predictable dramatic stall tactics. Mark Meadows put forth a hollow objection (he knew it was going nowhere) that the written testimony had come in too late the night before and therefore the proceedings should be delayed. That led to an opposing motion to table his objection, then a roll call vote that carried the motion, and the Democratic majority quashed the objection. But the stalling wasn't over. Ranking committee member Jim Jordan delivered a screed about our putting a convicted person under oath, hardly the first time this has been done in a court of law or in the Congress of the United States. Representative Jordan closed his rant with what he thought was a damning statement: "Mr. Chairman, your chairmanship will always be identified with this hearing. . . ." Well, I hope he's right. I'm not looking for glory, I'm looking for change. I hope what came out of this hearing in some way leads to a return to truth and perhaps some measure of justice.

Finally . . . finally we got down to the business of the hearing. I summarized what Mr. Cohen would cover, the highlights, or rather lowlights, of the Trump candidacy and presidency, the name-calling, denials, contradictions, and bald-faced lies. I left it to Michael Cohen to fill in the details and provide the evidence.

It is worth noting that our committee did not subpoena Michael Cohen. We could have; we have that right, but we did not. Based on his trial and prior testimony, we knew the substance of his message. He had been convicted. He would serve prison time. There was no more justice to be meted out for Michael Cohen.

In fact, he requested the opportunity to address the committee and the United States Congress. His lawyer, Lanny Davis, called me and said, "Michael wants to speak directly to the American people."

"Is he sure?" I asked. "He'll be badgered and berated and attacked with accusations and defamatory comments."

Davis went back to Cohen and asked him again. Again, Michael Cohen said he wanted to speak. He wanted a chance to tell the truth. So we arranged for him to appear before the committee on February 27, 2019.

In some ways it feels like ancient history now, but I tell it here in detail because the constant barrage of Trump offenses often bury each other to the point that with each new one we can hardly recall how outrageous the last one was. We become numb. But we can't. We shouldn't.

Before he read his prepared statement, I directly addressed the question on everyone's mind: Why should we believe Michael Cohen, a man who lied to Congress and lied to law enforcement about his actions to protect the president?

"Some will certainly ask," I said, "if Mr. Cohen was lying then, why should we believe him now? This is a legitimate question. As a trial lawyer for many years, I've faced this situation over and over again. And I asked the same question. Here is how I view our role. Every one of us in this room has a duty to serve as an independent check on the Executive Branch. Ladies and gentlemen, we are in search of the truth. The president has made many statements of his own, and now the American people have a right to hear the other side. They can watch Mr. Cohen's testimony and make their own judgment."

I banged the gavel and Michael Cohen addressed the committee and Congress: "I recognize that some of you may doubt and attack me on my credibility. It is for this reason that I have incorporated into this opening statement documents that are irrefutable, and demonstrate that the information you will hear is accurate and truthful. I am ashamed of my weakness and misplaced loyalty—of the things I did for Mr. Trump in an effort to protect and promote him. . . . I am ashamed because I know what Mr. Trump is. He is a racist. He is a con man. He is a cheat."

To Cohen's credit, he went right at the skepticism that might exist, as to why anyone should believe him, and he set out to build his case on facts. I may not respect him for what he did in defending Donald Trump all those years but I recognized a lawyer making a good case. He started with his own disarming confession: "Before going further, I want to apologize to each of you and to Congress. . . . The last time I appeared before Congress, I came to protect Mr. Trump. Today, I'm here to tell the truth about Mr. Trump. I lied to Congress about when Mr. Trump stopped negotiating the Moscow Tower project in Russia . . . that we stopped negotiating in January 2016. That was false. . . . To be clear: Mr. Trump knew of and directed the Trump Moscow negotiations throughout the campaign and lied about it. He lied about it because he never expected to win the election. He also lied about it because he stood to make hundreds of millions of dollars on the Moscow real estate project. And so I lied about it, too. . . ."

He admitted his own guilt, not broadly or dismissively, but in detail, effectively taking those issues off the table. "[L]ast fall I pled guilty in federal court to felonies for the benefit of, at the direction of, and in coordination with Individual #1. For the record: Individual #1 is President Donald J. Trump. It is painful to admit that I was motivated by ambition at times . . . many times I ignored my conscience and acted loyal to a man when I should not have. . . . I have come here to apologize to my family, to the government, and to the American people."

By this point, Cohen had even his harshest doubters glued to his words. His tale was as riveting as a Stephen King story; truth is truly stranger than fiction. "[L]et me now tell you about Mr. Trump. I got to know him very well, working very closely with him for more than 10 years. . . . When I first met Mr. Trump, he was a successful entrepreneur, a real estate giant, and an icon. . . . I wound up touting the Trump narrative for over a decade. . . . It monopolized my life. At first, I worked mostly on real estate developments and other business transactions. Shortly thereafter, Mr. Trump brought me into his personal life and private dealings. Over time, I saw his true character. . . . He has both good and bad, as do we all. But the bad far outweighs the good, and since taking office, he has become the worst version of himself. He is capable of behaving kindly, but he is not kind. He is capable of committing acts of generosity, but he is not generous. He is capable of being loyal, but he is fundamentally disloyal."

When Cohen described the president of the United States as

"fundamentally disloyal," that was a breathtaking phrase. Can the person who holds the position with the highest responsibility in the land be disloyal? To us? To those he represents? To his country? To the Constitution? There is probably no trait more fundamental to the office of the president than loyalty.

Cohen then dissected the president's motives and priorities, dismantling Trump's favorite refrain. "Donald Trump is a man who ran for office to make his brand great, not to make our country great. . . . Mr. Trump would often say, this campaign was going to be the 'greatest infomercial in political history.' He never expected to win the primary. He never expected to win the general election. The campaign—for him—was always a marketing opportunity." That cynical view made me cringe. I still believe in patriotism. So do my colleagues, I hope. The question was, would they believe Cohen's calling out the emperor's new clothes or would they choose to bury their heads in the sand?

Cohen connected the dots between Trump's business behavior and his White House ethics. "[E]arly on in my work for Mr. Trump he would direct me to lie to further his business interests. . . . I considered it trivial. As the President, I consider it significant and dangerous."

The opposition, the Republican stalwarts, grumbled and groaned. They were skeptical, expectedly, of his opinions and judgment. Who was Cohen to judge? But they couldn't help but listen to tawdry detail after tawdry detail. It was addictive. And if factually true, it should have caused revolt and abandoning the Trump ship. On the subject of whether Trump knew about the release of the hacked Democratic National Committee emails in advance, Cohen said, "The answer is yes. . . . In July 2016, days before the Democratic convention, I was in Mr. Trump's office when his secretary announced that Roger Stone was on the phone. . . . Mr. Stone told Mr. Trump that he had just gotten off the phone with Julian Assange and that Mr. Assange told Mr. Stone that, within a couple of days, there would be a massive dump of emails that would damage Hillary Clinton's campaign. Mr. Trump responded . . . to the effect of 'wouldn't that be great.'" On the subject of Trump's alleged racism, Cohen said, "You have heard him call poorer countries 'shitholes.' In private, he is even worse. He once asked me if I could name a country run by a black person that wasn't a 'shithole.' This was when Barack Obama was President. . . . While we were once driving through a struggling neighborhood in Chicago, he commented that only black people could live that way. And, he told me that black people would never vote for him because they were too stupid. And yet I continued to work for him."

On the subject of Trump's financial practices, Cohen provided hard evidence, financial statements—documents that had been almost impossible for us to get. "Mr. Trump is a cheat. . . . I'm giving the Committee today three years of President Trump's financial statements, from 2011–2013, which he gave to Deutsche Bank to inquire about a loan to buy the Buffalo Bills. . . . Mr. Trump inflated his total assets when it served his purposes, such as trying to be listed among the wealthiest people in *Forbes*, and deflated his assets to reduce his real estate taxes. . . . Mr. Trump directed me to call business owners . . . that were owed money for their services and told them no payment or a reduced payment would be coming." Cohen continued to fess up to his own culpability: "yet, I continued to work for him."

Then there was the infamous Stormy Daniels (Stephanie Clifford) story, lurid, sleazy, and dark. We had heard it before but it was like a car accident by the side of the road—you can't help but watch. To hear it told, firsthand, by the man who carried out the deeds was even more compelling. Cohen didn't just know about it. He did it. "Mr. Trump is a con man. He asked me to pay off an adult film star with whom he had an affair, and to lie to his wife about it. . . . Lying to the First Lady is one of my biggest regrets." Again, he provided documents, including "a copy of the $130,000 wire transfer from me to Ms. Clifford's attorney during the closing days of the presidential campaign that was demanded by Ms. Clifford to maintain her silence about her affair with Mr. Trump. . . ." He gave us detail upon detail: "Mr. Trump directed me to use my own personal funds from a Home Equity Line of Credit to avoid any money being traced back to him that could negatively impact his campaign. . . . I am going to jail in part because of my decision to help Mr. Trump hide that payment from the American people before they voted a few days later. . . . I am providing a copy of a $35,000 check that President Trump personally signed from his personal bank account on August 1, 2017—when he was President of the United States—pursuant to the cover-up, which was the basis of my guilty plea, to reimburse me . . . for the illegal hush money I paid on his behalf . . . part of a criminal scheme to violate campaign finance laws. . . ." More evidence. More confession.

Cohen even described actions and handiwork that weren't restricted to big business deals, but were just acts of vanity and thin skin. "When I say con man, I'm talking about a man who declares himself brilliant but directed me to threaten his high school, his colleges, and the College Board to never release his grades or SAT scores." Cohen gave us a copy of a letter he sent at Trump's direction threatening schools with civil and criminal actions if Trump's actual grades or SAT scores were disclosed.

Cohen repeated some of Trump's most awful statements, including the ugly dismissal of Republican icon, former presidential candidate, and war hero John McCain. "During the campaign, Mr. Trump said he did not consider Vietnam Veteran, and Prisoner of War, Senator John McCain to be 'a hero' because he likes people who weren't captured." Hypocritically, Cohen said that candidate Trump had him deflect negative press on his own medical deferment from the Vietnam draft. Trump claimed he had a bone spur, but when Cohen asked for medical records, there were none. He just said, "You think I'm stupid, I wasn't going to Vietnam." (Again, Cohen's sad confession,) "And yet, I continued to work for him."

I was torn between feeling sick to my stomach at the way the president behaved and was treating his country and feeling pity for this man who had done his bidding, who had sold his own soul for money and momentary power.

I thought his next statement was remarkably candid and open. As much as he now despised his former boss, he did not make accusations he couldn't back up. He told only what he knew, and I think that added to his credibility. I provide his own words and let others judge. "Questions have been raised about whether I know of direct evidence that Mr. Trump or his campaign colluded with Russia. I do not. . . . But, I have my suspicions. . . . I remember being in the room with Mr. Trump, probably in early June 2016, when something peculiar happened. Don Jr.

came into the room and walked behind his father's desk . . . leaning over to his father and speaking in a low voice, which I could clearly hear, and saying: 'The meeting is all set.' I remember Mr. Trump saying, 'Ok good . . . let me know.' What struck me . . . was, first, that Mr. Trump had frequently told me and others that his son Don Jr. had the worst judgment of anyone in the world. And also, that Don Jr. would never set up any meeting of any significance alone—and certainly not without checking with his father. . . . So, I concluded that Don Jr. was referring to that June 2016 Trump Tower meeting about dirt on Hillary with the Russian representative. . . ." Did Trump collude? Was he a knowing partner in the actions? Or was it a perfectly innocent exchange between father and son?

Finally, after so many hours, Michael Cohen ended on a very human, personally vulnerable note. He repeated what Trump had said that created a very real threat to Cohen in prison. He shared his fears for his life. Anyone, Democrat, Republican, independent, any human being could relate to that fear. "To you, Chairman Cummings, Ranking Member Jordan, the other members of this Committee, and the other members of the House and Senate, I am sorry for my lies and for lying to Congress . . . for actively working to hide from you the truth about Mr. Trump when you needed it most. . . . My testimony certainly does not diminish the pain I caused my family and friends. . . . And I have never asked for, nor would I accept, a pardon from President Trump. . . . Mr. Trump called me a 'rat' for choosing to tell the truth—much like a mobster would do when one of his men decides to cooperate with the government. . . . I have provided the Committee with copies of Tweets that Mr. Trump posted, attacking me and my family . . . encouragement to someone to do harm to me and my family. . . . I am not a perfect man. I have done things I am not proud of, and I will live with the consequences of my actions for the rest of my life. But today, I get to decide the example I set for my children and how I attempt to change how history will remember me. I may not be able to change the past, but I can do right by the American people here today. Thank you."

It was one of the most powerful events I have been witness to in my almost seven decades of life. Hour after hour, the committee members grilled Cohen. They asked him every imaginable question in every form. Some challenged his credibility and motives. Some questioned his honesty. Some applauded his willingness to speak. Some delivered rants against him. But no matter what form the questions took, no matter how fact-driven or ego-driven, prosecutorial or partisan, objective or biased, or just plain grandstanding, over and over, all he did was what he swore to do. He told the truth.

Some of the best questions came from some of the youngest, newest members of Congress: Ayanna Pressley (Massachusetts), Rashida Tlaib (Michigan), Katie Hill (California), and Alexandria Ocasio-Cortez (New York), the so-called Squad of young, newly elected firebrands in Congress. Ocasio-Cortez dove right into the *National Enquirer* stories that had been squashed through the "catch and kill" method (the publication buys the story in order to *not* run it, to protect the subject of the story from embarrassment)—like adult film star Stormy Daniels's allegations. Cohen said he did not know where the documents related to "catch and kill" were. So Ocasio-Cortez asked Cohen where the committee could learn more about the documents and Cohen listed David Pecker, Barry Levine, and Dylan Howard. (Pecker is CEO of American Media, *National Enquirer*'s parent; Levine is a former *National Enquirer* editor and Howard is a vice president of American Media.) She kept going—digging into accusations that Trump overstated his net worth when it helped him—that is, to make a large purchase—and understated it when it helped him—that is, to reduce taxes. Cohen said he knew Trump did that but said he couldn't provide details. So Ocasio-Cortez did as she did with the *National Enquirer* questions; she asked where else the committee might go to gain information on this tactic. "Do you think we need to review his [Trump's] financial statements and tax returns in order to compare them?" "Would it help for the committee to obtain federal and state tax returns from the president and his company to address that discrepancy?" Michael Cohen agreed on both questions and he offered names of people who might know more: Trump Organization associates Allen Weisselberg, Ron Lieberman, and Matthew Calamari. Her questions gave the committee and Congress specific paths to pursue.

In stark contrast to the serious inquiries, Paul Gosar, Republican of Arizona, said Cohen was a "disgraced lawyer," not to be believed, and went after him with a line most of us hadn't heard since grade school, "Liar, liar, pants on fire." More relevantly, his Republican colleague James Comer of Kentucky said to Cohen, if President Trump is a "cheat," what does that make him (Cohen)? And Cohen replied, "a fool." Jim Jordan of Ohio, the ranking Republican on the committee, said that the witness's "remorse is minimal, his instinct to blame others is strong." Cohen responded, "I plead guilty and take responsibility for my actions. Shame on you, Mr. Jordan."

At one point, when the accusations and attacks were especially rough from the Republicans, Cohen said, "I find it interesting that not one question from you today has been about Mr. Trump. That's why I thought I was coming today."

Then Justin Amash, a Michigan Republican at the time who since split from the party as a declared libertarian, spoke. He said he wasn't sure we should trust Michael Cohen. But then he asked a thoughtful question that literally left Cohen nearly silent. "What is the truth that you know President Trump fears most?" Cohen didn't answer quickly. He thought. And thought. And then said, "That's a tough question, sir. I don't have an answer for that." His non-answer—the idea that it was hard to even conceive of the worst thing Trump had done—was as chilling as any fact or story he had revealed all day.

The truth. Seven-plus hours of the truth as best Michael Cohen could recall it. It was sobering truth. It was terrifying truth. In many ways he told us what we already knew—the president's prejudice and duplicity, the denials, arrogance, scheming, and disregard for, or ignorance of, the laws and values of America. He added new stories, new horrors, repugnant details, and sordid anecdotes. In total, it was ugly undeniable truth. And throughout it all, we had to keep reminding ourselves, we were not just hearing an attorney tell us about some bad guy client; this client was the president of the United States.

By the end of the day, personally, I had had a transformative experience. The reality, which I may have known piece by piece, hit me full force. It was literally staggering. I saw on the faces of my colleagues, even those who publicly supported the president, that the reality of this man and his values, or vacuum of values, was unprecedented. We had a leader of our country who had no moral center. It was my job to close the hearing. I had to gather my thoughts and deliver a conclusion, some level of wisdom and perspective after a day of revealing shameful, reprehensible, almost unspeakable behavior and beliefs.

I started with my sympathy, even empathy, for Michael Cohen. "I've listened to all this, and it's very painful. It's very painful. You made a lot of mistakes, Mr. Cohen—and you've admitted that." You cannot witness something like this and not feel at least a little for this man, bad as his deeds might have been, because now he will be suffering and so will his family. But there is more to this man than a confession, an admission. There is the possibility of change. I saw Cohen as a man at a crossroads, like so many I had seen before. "When I practiced law I represented a lot of lawyers who got in trouble. And, you come saying I have made my mistakes, but now I want to change my life. . . . If we . . . as a nation did not give people an opportunity after they've made mistakes to change their lives, a whole lot of people would not do very well." I wanted to remind my friends and adversaries in Congress, and anyone and everyone watching, that we are a country of second chances. We were founded as a second chance—so many people forget our history. I wanted people to look at these deeds and schemes and values in perspective, to refuse and reject and refute them as not us, not America, not who we are. I wanted people to declare, loud and clear, as I did at that moment, *"We are better than this. We really are. As a country, we are so much better than this."*

I offered Mr. Cohen that same advice I repeat to my children and often to myself when faced with adversity. "When bad things happen to you, do not ask the question 'Why did it happen *to* me?' Ask the question, 'Why did it happen *for* me?' I don't know why this is happening for you. But it's my hope that a small part of it is for our country to be better." I retold the story of my one and only meeting with President Trump when I said to him "the greatest gift you and I . . . can give to our children is . . . a democracy that is intact," because it was my hope that what we had all witnessed that day would help us keep our democracy intact. Did I believe it? In the long term, yes. But for now I could only hope. Because, as I told the audience, according to the *Washington Post*, at that point the president had told thousands of untrue statements (a fraction of what he managed to amass as time has gone on). Is that what we want to teach our children? No. But Mr. Cohen, and others, got caught up in it. It's contagious. And lethal.

There was something else I wanted to address directly: the prospect of prison. Michael Cohen was testifying to us that day, in a nice business suit, in a big open room, with a pitcher of ice water and lunch served and all the amenities of society. But soon he would be behind bars, far from the amenities of society. I knew that consequence well, from my law practice, from clients who became convicts and faced a change that most of us cannot fathom. It is a place with its own rules and labels and punishments. The president of the United States called Michael Cohen a "rat." I know that term well. It isn't just a rodent that roots through trash. It's one of the worst things you can call somebody because "when they go to prison, that means a snitch." And you will pay for that in prison.

Again, I exhorted anyone listening, *"We're better than that! We really are."* I hoped in my soul that we could get back to the democracy we want, the democracy we should be passing on to our children, who hopefully will do better than we did.

Would people believe Michael Cohen? That was the question on all of our minds, regardless of party. Why believe him? He was hardly a role model, but rather just an ambitious man who gave in to his lesser instincts. But I had seen one moment that I could not shake, that I wanted to share, to make sure others saw, "the picture that really, really pained me. You were leaving the prison, you were leaving the courthouse, and, I guess it's your daughter, had braces or something on [a crutch after hip surgery]. Man, that thing, man, that thing hurt me. As a father of two daughters, it hurt me." That alone isn't a reason to believe Michael Cohen. But it is a reason to think that he is a human being who hurts. Who got up in front of Congress and confessed to inexcusable acts. Who let his daughter see him in his worst light . . . maybe so she could have a better view of him as he went off to serve his penance.

I then thanked Mr. Cohen. Yes, I thanked him because what he did was hard. He didn't have to do it but he chose to. I tried to assure him that this was a part of his destiny, that might lead to "a better Michael Cohen, a better Donald Trump, a better United States of America, and a better world." I meant that from the depths of my heart.

And I meant my closing words with all of my soul. *"When we're dancing with the angels, the question we'll be asked: In 2019, what did we do to make sure we kept our democracy intact?* Did we stand on the sidelines and say nothing?" I adjourned the meeting.

Cummings family portrait, from left: Elijah's older brother, Robert Jr.; father, Robert Sr.; older sister, Cheretheria; mother, Ruth; and Elijah, at the time the baby of the family.
Courtesy of Yvonne Cummings

Older brother Elijah and his younger brother James
Courtesy of Yvonne Cummings

Elijah and his younger brothers Carnel and James

Elijah, looking up to his older brother Robert Jr.
Courtesy of Yvonne Cummings

Elijah's high school photo—City College of Baltimore High School
Courtesy of Yvonne Cummings

U.S. Congressman
Parren Mitchell,
Delegate Lena
King Lee, and
Elijah Cummings at
Maryland House of
Delegates
Courtesy of the
Moorland-Spingarn
Research Center at
Howard University

Elijah Cummings at a meeting with
U.S. Senator Paul Sarbanes, U.S.
House Speaker Tip O'Neill, and
U.S. Congressman Parren Mitchell
Courtesy of the Moorland-Spingarn
Research Center at Howard University

Elijah with Juanita Jackson
Mitchell, the attorney and civil
rights pioneer who inspired him
to become a lawyer
Courtesy of the Moorland-Spingarn
Research Center at Howard University

Maya Rockeymoore,
President Bill Clinton,
First Lady Hillary
Clinton, and Elijah
at a White House
Christmas party, 2000
White House photographer

Elijah Cummings;
President George W. Bush;
Dorothy I. Height, head
of the National Council of
Negro Women; Speaker
Dennis Hastert. Ms.
Height is receiving the
Congressional Gold Medal
from President Bush.

Senator Barack Obama,
Senator John Kerry, and
Elijah Cummings during
Kerry's 2004 run for
president
Maya Rockeymoore Cummings

Nancy Pelosi and
Elijah Cummings in
Washington, DC

Senator John McCain
and Elijah Cummings
backstage at CBS before
a news show, April 2014

Elijah Cummings and Maya Rockeymoore Cummings's vow renewal ceremony, December 2011
Kevin Brown

"The kiss." Elijah and Maya's vow renewal ceremony, December 2011
Kevin Brown

Maya and Elijah
with Eric Holder
and his wife,
Sharon Malone, at
the White House
Correspondents
Dinner

Jesse Jackson Sr.
and Elijah at the
Congressional
Black Caucus
Foundation
annual legislative
conference
*Maya Rockeymoore
Cummings*

President Barack
Obama, Vice
President Joe
Biden, and Elijah
Cummings at the
White House
*White House
photographer*

Elijah and his older daughter,
Jennifer Cummings
Courtesy Jennifer Cummings

Elijah and his younger daughter, Adia
Cummings, at M&T Bank Stadium for a
Baltimore Ravens football game
Maya Rockeymoore Cummings

Elijah Cummings, Vice President Biden, and Jennifer Cummings at
Washington, DC, event
Courtesy Jennifer Cummings

Elijah in the Congressional hearing room of the U.S. House, now named the Elijah E. Cummings Hearing Room
Jack Gruber/USA TODAY NETWORK

Wolf Blitzer and Elijah Cummings at Howard University commencement in 2014
Maya Rockeymoore Cummings

Elijah Cummings speaking with then–New Jersey Governor Chris Christie

U.S. Speaker John Boehner,
Maya, and Elijah at Elijah's
swearing-in ceremony for the
U.S. House, January 2015
House photographer

Elijah Cummings, calming the
citizens, speaking to reporters
at the corner of Pennsylvania
and North Avenues during
the Freddie Gray unrest in
Baltimore City, April 2015
Maya Rockeymoore Cummings

Secretary of State Madeleine
Albright and Elijah
Cummings at the 2013
White House Correspondents
Dinner
Maya Rockeymoore Cummings

Elijah Cummings and U.S. Congressman
John Lewis, often called Elijah's "twin,"
as even the press mixed them up, in South
Africa for Nelson Mandela's funeral
Congressman Bobby Scott

Newt Gingrich and Elijah Cummings in
the green room of *Face the Nation*
Staff photographer

Maya, President Obama, and Elijah at a Bethesda fundraiser
DCC photographer

Maya, First Lady Michelle Obama, and Elijah at the Baltimore City
War Memorial at an Anthony Brown for Governor rally in 2014

Between First Lady Michelle Obama and President Barack Obama, daughters Jennifer and Adia flanking Elijah Cummings, at White House Christmas party
White House photographer

Elijah Cummings and his mother, Ruth Cummings, with President Barack Obama at a Baltimore event
White House photographer

Elijah Cummings and Maxine Waters celebrating in the U.S. Capitol on January 21, 2013, the day of Barack Obama's second inauguration
Maya Rockeymoore Cummings

Speaker Nancy Pelosi, Maya, and Elijah Cummings at his swearing-in ceremony, 2019
Staff photographer

Elijah Cummings speaking to members of the Howard University Choir in downtown Washington, DC
Maya Rockeymoore Cummings

Elijah Cummings's coffin being lifted up the steps of Statuary Hall in the U.S. Capitol, October 24, 2019
Jack Gruber/USA TODAY NETWORK

Speaker Pelosi bids Elijah Cummings a solemn farewell as Senate Majority Leader Mitch McConnell looks on during the lying-in-state ceremony in Statuary Hall
Jackie Hicks

President Obama hands Maya a tissue at Elijah's homegoing service at New Psalmist Baptist Church in Baltimore, October 25, 2019.
Jackie Hicks

Elijah E. Cummings was buried at Loudon Park Cemetery in Baltimore City with full military honors, October 25, 2019.
Jackie Hicks

A soldier presents the U.S. flag that had been draped over Elijah's coffin to his widow, Maya, at the gravesite, October 25, 2019.
Jackie Hicks

The hearing got a blanket of media coverage. It was chopped into juicy sound bites and played for days. Cable news, from MSNBC, to CNN, to Fox, traded punches on whether what he said was the exposure indictment of an unapologetic con man in chief or just sour grapes from a convict. My closing comments went viral. Facebook, YouTube, Instagram, Twitter, blogs, posts and reposts. Everywhere I went, I heard people saying, "Yes, Elijah, we are better than this." Regardless of where you are on the political spectrum, America got a full day of the truth. Will it be the beginning of more truth and ultimately change? I prayed that it would be. I prayed that I would be up to the challenge.

THERE ARE MOMENTS, I confess, when I am amazed to see my own growth as a person, as an elected official, as a servant of the people. I can recall, as if it was yesterday, a time when I would attend a press conference with other members of Congress and think to myself, What do I have to say? What do I have to offer that matters? The others seem to all know what to do. What am I doing here?

I would freeze up and let others speak—they seemed so eloquent. When the press conference was finally over, I'd just go home. I would tell my wife, Maya, about it, how I froze, and she'd remind me that my thoughts and opinions were unique; they were mine, from my heart, from my constituents, my streets, and my life. She'd say, "Tell them. Tell them what you know, what you've seen, what you feel." So I pushed myself. I'd step forward and open my mouth and I'd will the words to come out. You might say, I'd fake it until it was real. I discovered I did have something to say. I did have the experiences and the ideas that people wanted to hear. The reluctance began to disappear. Pretty soon other people were quoting me. They'd say, "As Elijah Cummings said . . ."

So when a day comes along like the day Michael Cohen spoke the truth in the face of doubters and enemies, in the glare of hot lights and cameras, under the threats of a president, and someone has to take the lead, I look back to the single experience, the moment that shaped me more than any other in my life. What in life prepared me for that day? My parents? Yes. My faith? Yes. But sometimes there is one shaping, formative, lasting, indelible event that you may not even realize is occurring when it happens, that forges your character into who you will become. I believe in my heart of hearts, in my soul, that it was something that happened to me as a young child. It prepared me for my life, and for a moment like this one. I want to take people not just to common ground, but to higher ground. That is what this moment in time did for me. That is how it shaped me.

When I was no more than eleven years old, my life was forever altered. I certainly didn't realize it at the time. I knew something important was happening but it took a long while before the impact really hit me.

We had a neighborhood community playground center where the kids would gather in the summer, with a small wading pool, and some recreation counselors to watch over us. My sister would make sure we younger kids had breakfast and then we'd go spend our day at the center, playing baseball or checkers, getting in the pool, or just hanging out with the other kids. One of the rec leaders was a guy named Jim Smith, who was also involved with the NAACP. Our little wading pool was no more than a few feet across and very shallow, maybe up to your knees and filled with kids, side by side. You had to take turns, a half hour at a time, and after the third group, the water was pretty dirty. But that was the only way we had to get cool on a hot day.

One day in late August, a lady came and asked us kids, "How would you like to go to a real swimming pool, one with a diving board, an Olympic-size pool?" We all thought that would be great but how was that going to happen? She said there was a pool like that only a few blocks away from where we were, in Riverside Park, that we deserved to go there, and she was going to take us. She said, "You can swim to your heart's delight." Those were her words almost fifty years ago: "to your heart's delight."

Her name was Juanita Jackson Mitchell. To us she was just the nice lady who was going to take us to a real swimming pool. We didn't realize until later that she was a civil rights pioneer from a family of civil rights pioneers and the first African-American woman to practice law in Maryland. Juanita Jackson Mitchell's mother was the inspirational Dr. Lillie Jackson, who descended from a signer of the Declaration of Independence, but still had to attend the segregated Colored High School, the Normal School "for the education of colored teachers," and became a second-grade teacher. She then rose to president of the Baltimore branch of the NAACP, became an early leader in nonviolent protest, and was known as the "Mother of Freedom." Her daughter, Juanita, was married to Clarence Mitchell Jr., a national leader in civil rights and lobbyist for the NAACP, and they were the parents of two state senators, Michael and Clarence III. Civil rights was practically the family business.

What Mrs. Mitchell did not tell us that day about the nice pool she was taking us to was that it was totally segregated, no blacks allowed. She and her colleagues at the rec center, Jim Smith and Walter Black, were leading us on an integration march. There we were, a band of little kids walking down the streets of Baltimore, from a black neighborhood to a white neighborhood, only a few blocks from each other, but worlds apart. Day after day, Juanita and Jim and Walter led about thirty of us, walking ten or fifteen blocks while an angry mob, not of other kids but grown white adults, yelled names at us, told us to go home, and threw rocks and bricks—at little kids. One of those rocks struck me in the forehead and caused a scar that I carry to this day. The police watched and the newspapers took pictures and ran stories but nobody stopped the angry residents . . . and nobody stopped us.

Walter Black, who was inspired by these events to go on to law school and then work for the NAACP, today lives on Maryland's Eastern Shore, and can still recount the incident. He says it began on August 28, when the leaders planned the event; then on the twenty-ninth they went to visit the pool site, and led the first marches to the pool on August 30 and 31, and September 1 and 2. We kids would swim in the Riverside Park pool each day, then leave, with "neighbors" yelling racial epithets and throwing debris and bottles and white kids pushing black kids in the pool. (I call them neighbors ironically. Yes, we all lived within blocks of each other, but they were hardly neighborly. They were the opposite, people trying to keep us out of their neighborhood.) Tensions were high. After taking Sunday off, they led us all back again on Monday, Labor Day, September 3. That day someone called Walter's associate Lyle Roberts a "nigger," and with the hostility escalating, the police urged the NAACP leaders to ride out of the area in a police wagon for their "safety," which they resisted but eventually agreed to.

About that time, the Riverside Park citizens, clinging to their segregated white enclave, must have realized that we were all going to just keep coming back, because they stopped coming to their doorways and out into the streets, shouting and throwing rocks. Just as Juanita Mitchell promised, we all got to go to a "real pool" and as she said, we swam "to our heart's delight." Even as little children we had a sense of victory—victory and fear. We'd gone off to play every day, but we ended up making history. Amazingly, nobody got seriously hurt.

This was in the early 1960s and old rules and practices and even prejudices began, slowly but steadily, to change. Baltimore stayed largely segregated for the next ten years but it was the beginning, the root of what would evolve into a massive upheaval in social norms—change.

For me, that was the beginning of wanting to become somebody who could make things change. I saw that Mitchell and the other people who made integration happen were lawyers. So I wanted to be a lawyer. These lawyers were young men and women who had the courage to walk up the streets and have people yell at them and be unafraid. To have little kids following them, trusting and believing in them. To make change happen. I wasn't sure what a lawyer was, what their job was, but I saw what they could accomplish. Oh my God, what a powerful force that could be. Change. Little black children getting what only white children had because we were, after all, just kids, no matter what color, who wanted the same chances in life, the chance to swim in a pool, the chance to go to a good school, or live in a nice neighborhood, or see a better world. I wanted to be part of that change. And I have endeavored to do so ever since. And I have pursued it ever since.

As for progress in achieving change, here is a fitting postscript: thirty years later, a man came up and identified himself as one of those in the angry mob and told me he was sorry. What is the right response to justice acknowledged but so long delayed? I did not applaud his admission. Nor did I spurn it. I said, "Apology accepted."

When I first went into my practice I became a lawyer for folks in my neighborhood, for a couple buying a first home, for young men in trouble, for families about to be evicted, for people battling bill collectors, for kids who wanted to go to college, for small businesses. I worked my way up to larger cases, but what they all had in common was people, my clients, who needed someone on their side to help to get what they were entitled to. They needed help to get fairness.

Now, these many years later, many unlikely events later, from neighborhood advocate to the state legislature to the U.S. Congress to the Oversight Committee, my moment had come to be a lawyer for the whole country. Because sometimes even a country needs help to get what's fair.

IN *ALL THE PRESIDENT'S MEN*, the movie about the Watergate break-in, the line "Follow the money" was attributed to Deep Throat, the anonymous source who eventually led reporters and investigators to the true story behind how Nixon and his team broke into Democratic headquarters to get inside information on the election plans. If there ever was a second case of "follow the money," Michael Cohen's testimony was it. He gave us a road map to follow and to reveal possible wrong-doing by the president. Cohen's description of how Donald Trump routinely inflated and deflated his income and net worth reopened questions about whether he personally, or through his businesses, had jeopardized the security of the country through deals with financial institutions, investors, or leaders of foreign governments. Cohen's colorful story of Trump's effort to buy the Buffalo Bills NFL team was just one such business example. (Trump claimed a sudden jump in net worth of over $4 billion, but even so, the NFL rejected his bid.) The specter of bank dealings, domestic and overseas, that might reveal improper agreements, compromised confidentiality, or quid pro quo promises all loomed large. We've all heard of the smell test—well, this trail stunk to the high heavens. We had more than good reason to review Trump's financial records but, until this time, he had blocked all efforts to get his tax returns or other financial documents. Shortly after the hearing, our committee prepared a letter to Victor Wahba, the CEO of accounting firm Mazars USA LLP, requesting ten years of Trump records. The letter referenced Michael Cohen's sworn testimony, and we were crystal clear as to what we wanted and why.

On February 27, 2019, the President's former attorney, Michael Cohen, testified before the Committee that President Trump changed the estimated value of his assets and liabilities on financial statements prepared by your company. . . .

. . . Mr. Cohen testified that President Trump provided inflated financial statements "to Deutsche Bank on one occasion where I was with them in our attempt to obtain money so we can put a bid on the Buffalo Bills." . . . Mr. Cohen further testified that President Trump may have deflated certain assets to "reduce his real estate taxes." He explained, "What you do is you deflate the value of an asset, and then you put in a request to the tax department for a deduction."

Our letter then asked for documentation to account for the president's net worth skyrocketing in one year, June 2012 to March 2013, by $4.2 billion, with the bulk of the valuation attributed to "brand value." Further, we asked for details on the omission from his financial records of $75 million in debt on Chicago property and assets in Las Vegas valued at over $50 million. We asked for documents to explain debts and liabilities, including whether Trump owed money to a Korean conglomerate that was dissolved after a corruption investigation involving Deutsche Bank. We asked for records to justify an interest on a loan from Deutsche Bank that was reduced far below market rate immediately after Trump became a presidential candidate.

We spelled out what records and underlying documents we wanted—any and all related to Donald J. Trump, Donald J. Trump Revocable Trust, the Trump Organization LLC, the Trump Corporation, DJT Holdings LLC, the Trump Post Office LLC, the Trump Foundation and related entities, as well as any communications between Donald Bender (the Mazars principal handling the Trump matters) and Donald Trump or employees of the Trump Organization. We closed the letter by reminding the accounting firm of our authority in such matters, to request, and if need be, demand the information:

> The Committee on Oversight and Reform is the principal
> oversight committee of the House of Representatives and
> has broad authority to investigate "any matter" at "any time"
> under House Rule X . . . conducting oversight of Government
> activities at all levels, including the Executive Office of the
> President.

And I signed the letter. But before it could even be mailed, two Republican members of the committee sent me their own letter, assailing the legitimate purpose of the committee's request. Jim Jordan and Mark Meadows said that just asking for this information "appears to depart from responsible and legitimate oversight . . . solely to embarrass President Trump and to advance relentless Democrat attacks upon the Trump administration." They went on, "We should not waste our limited resources and energies on matters that do not improve the operations of the federal government or better the lives of our constituents. . . ."

Even that wasn't enough for them. They sent a letter directly to Victor Wahba, CEO of Mazars, complaining that I didn't consult with them as minority members before asking his firm for the documents. Really? Really, Mr. Jordan and Mr. Meadows? Come on. Were you not in the House of Representatives during Michael Cohen's testimony? Did you not hear his specific references to incidents and records documenting those incidents? Did you think we, the Oversight Committee, should just say, "Oh, that's too bad. Presidents shouldn't do that. We'll ask Mr. Trump not to do any more of that"? Let's not forget the full name of our committee—Oversight *and* Reform. We're not here just to watch what's going on; we're here to correct it when it's wrong! I wasted no time and minced no words when the media asked me about what Jordan and Meadows had done. "If they had their way, the committee would just close up shop for the next two years, but that is not what the American people elected us to do." "We are following up on specific allegations regarding the president's actions based on corroborating documents obtained by the committee. . . . [They] complain about every single thing I do. We're just seeking the truth, that's all."

That wasn't the end of the melodrama. The president himself hadn't weighed in yet. I had often said during this time that I was a little surprised the president hadn't tweeted about me yet. I don't know why he hadn't gone after me with his bullying Twitter thumbs yet, but he hadn't. Maybe it was because of our first meeting. Maybe it was out of some sort of respect. That first conversation had been very real; it gave him a chance to see how I am, and that I can see through his BS, that I hate what he's doing and he knows it. He's gone after lots of people but not many have gone after him harder than I have. I figured what I was doing now—subpoenaing eight years of his financial records—might push him over the edge and he'd hit back with his tweets. But he didn't.

Instead he sued me. Technically he sued the committee, but me personally as well, as committee chair. He got a clear indication of how hard I would pursue him when we demanded the documents. He probably didn't fully understand that we had the right to the documents. He filed suits to stop Mazars from giving the documents to us. And he singled me out, by name, in the suit. To tell the truth, it was like a badge of honor. It bothered him so much, he evidently had so much to hide, he sued to stop it. His lawyers filed suit in federal district court asserting that I, Committee Chair Elijah E. Cummings, had no legitimate basis to subpoena the accounting firm. Even the complaint itself was inflammatory. "The Democrat Party, with its newfound control of the U.S. House of Representatives, has declared all-out political war against President Donald J. Trump. Subpoenas are their weapon of choice." Speaking of weapons of choice, suing was Trump's go-to move from his real estate days. According to *USA Today*, Trump and his various ventures had filed more than four thousand lawsuits on everything from defamation to trademark infringement to employment issues, with the idea that a vicious lawsuit could sometimes intimidate the other side enough.

On the Monday of the filing, his attorney Jay Sekulow said, "We will not allow congressional presidential harassment to go unanswered." On the same day, I said the lawsuit was no surprise considering Trump's "long history of trying to use baseless lawsuits to attack adversaries," but Trump did not have any "valid legal basis to interfere with this duly authorized subpoena from Congress." Sorry, but when it comes to intimidation with the hope of us backing off—he had the wrong guy, on the wrong issue.

On May 20, U.S. District Court judge Amit Mehta, in a forty-one-page opinion, rejected their argument and supported our authority to investigate. He wrote: "So long as Congress investigates on a subject matter on which 'legislation could be had,'" we were well within our constitutional duties and rights. He flatly stated, "President Trump cannot block the subpoena to Mazars." He even went so far as to say that other important congressional probes—such as Watergate—might never have happened if the argument of Trump's lawyers was valid. I cheered the decision, a "resounding victory for the rule of law." I added, "The court recognized the basic, but crucial fact that Congress has authority to conduct investigations as part of our core function under the Constitution" and "The court rejected President Trump's repeated claim that congressional investigations serve no 'legislative function,'" an argument he had lobbed at several other investigations by the House.

Of course, Trump didn't say, "Okay, here are the records." He called the ruling "crazy" and said he'd appeal it, another go-to move/threat/promise from his past arsenal. And he had one more reflex response. Trump said, "As far as the financials are concerned, it's totally the wrong decision [by an] Obama-appointed judge." When in doubt, bring up Barack or Hillary. Nonetheless, we had won the round. Now on to the appeals. We knew we'd likely end up in court after court in our process. As they say, the wheels of justice grind slowly.

On October 11, 2019, the United States Court of Appeals for the District of Columbia Circuit ruled 2 to 1 to affirm the earlier, lower court ruling by the federal district court judge that Trump's accounting firm must yield to the Oversight Committee's demand for eight years of financial records. Writing the majority opinion, Judge David Tatel stated, "A congressional committee, as committees have done repeatedly over the past two centuries, issued an investigative subpoena, and the target of that subpoena, questioning the committee's legislative purpose, has asked a court to invalidate it. . . . The fact that the subpoena in this case seeks information that concerns the president of the United States adds a twist, but not a surprising one." He went on to conclude, "We detect no inherent constitutional flaw in laws requiring presidents to publicly disclose certain financial information. And that is enough."

Amen. I shouted for joy! Of course, the statement I issued was more measured: "Today's ruling is a fundamental and resounding victory for congressional oversight, our constitutional system of checks and balances and the rule of law. For far too long, the president has placed his personal interests over the interests of the American people." Nancy Pelosi weighed in via a letter to all Democrats in the House: "The president's actions threaten our national security, violate our Constitution and undermine the integrity of our elections. No one is above the law. The president will be held accountable."

Of course, Trump's lawyers didn't admit defeat. Jay Sekulow reviewed the decision and issued a statement saying, "We continue to believe that this subpoena is not a legitimate exercise of Congress's legislative authority." What that means is that the president and his attorneys can still appeal to the Supreme Court but it is rare that any court, including the Supreme Court, has blocked Congress's right to issue subpoenas. Is it over? Hardly.

"WE THE PEOPLE . . ." are the first three words of the United States Constitution. Any school kid knows that, or used to, when civics was taught in every school. It's worth a reminder:

We the people of the United States, in Order to form a more perfect Union, establish Justice, insure domestic Tranquility, provide for the common defence, promote the general Welfare, and secure the Blessings of Liberty to ourselves and our Posterity, do ordain and establish this Constitution for the United States of America.

Those words are not to be taken for granted. I am reminding anyone who reads this book because those words are important to your life and freedom every single day!

I remind myself of them every time I set foot on the floor of the House of Representatives. I tell my staff members, if you work for me, you need to know the Constitution, the collection of "rules" we follow, the basic principles that set the United States apart from the monarchy we had overthrown in our revolution. We rejected the arbitrary rule of one person, a king or queen, not elected or voted or agreed upon, but chosen by birth and blood. We chose to rule ourselves. We chose to vote for our leaders. We chose a balance or separation of powers in three coequal branches of government to prevent one branch from having absolute rule over the others. We had rebelled against a monarchy and were guarding against another one. Article I (Legislative branch), Section 1 of the Constitution states: "All legislative Powers herein granted shall be vested in a Congress of the United States, which shall consist of a Senate and House of Representatives." Article II (Executive branch), Section 1 states: "The executive Power shall be vested in a President of the United States of America.

He shall hold his Office during the term of four Years, and together with the Vice President, chosen for the same term, be elected. . . ." Article III (Judicial branch), Section 1 states: "The judicial Power of the United States, shall be vested in one supreme Court, and such inferior Courts as the Congress may from time to time ordain and establish."

Those aren't just words for school kids to memorize and recite. There's a lot in there worth all of us understanding: Three branches, not one. Legislative power resides in the Congress, that is the creation of the laws, all laws. Congress has two houses—more balance. Executive power resides in the president, who is elected. For four years at a time—not for life like a monarch—more balance. Judicial power resides in the Supreme Court—to rule on the law, the actions of the president. Additional courts are established by Congress—more balance.

I am reminding readers of these tenets, but I am also reminding one other person: the president of the United States, Donald J. Trump. You are elected. For a four-year term. Two terms maximum. You do not have congressional power. Or judicial power. You hold the power you do have at the will of the people.

We have a system of checks and balances. It's good because it prevents one branch from overpowering any other. Our form of governance maintains the will of the people. But it can be slow. Painfully slow. When one branch does something another branch disagrees with, the process requires review by one of the other branches, by the checks and balances built into our government. It takes a lot of patience to do government work, especially to do it openly and fairly, with balance, without the mandate of a king or emperor or dictator, but instead the way our founding fathers and the Constitution intended. But it works. It is fair and just. In the words of Martin Luther King, "The arc of the moral universe is long, but it bends towards justice." Let it be true.

CHAPTER 5

Chasing Truth

Following the Cohen hearings and the groundwork they laid, the Oversight Committee set out on a series of nonstop investigations of the Trump administration's relentless and reckless disregard for precedent, decency, or law.

A shorthand version of our calendar of hearings read: Blocked access to documents from the Departments of Justice, Homeland Security, Health and Human Services; failure to address the opioid crisis; lack of transparency in the administration; the 2020 Census and the attempt to add a vote-suppressing citizenship question; climate change inaction/denial and rollbacks; immigration policy of child separation; veterans and active-duty military suicides; confronting white supremacy; health care for veterans; violations of the Hatch Act (in particular Kellyanne Conway); embargo of documents from the FBI, GSA, and Office of Personnel Management; the administration's attack on the Affordable Care Act; immigration again on kids in cages and inhumane treatment at the border; lessons after Hurricane Maria; immigration yet again on Homeland Security under Acting Secretary Kevin McAleenan; vaping and the nicotine epidemic; skyrocketing drug prices; deportation of critically ill children and families; Syria policy; and even the extravagant cost of the administration's self-promoting Fourth of July parade.

We were out of breath trying to keep up. We all felt the immense, unabated urgency and pressure. The American public had entrusted us to be the check on this president that had been absent for two years. With the next election only two years away, we knew we had a limited window to achieve meaningful progress. We had to set priorities—even in a tidal wave of disasters, some more disastrous than others.

In March 2019, the committee began a series of hearings on the upcoming 2020 U.S. Census and the attempt by the Commerce Department to add a question about citizenship. It might seem to be innocent, maybe even sensible, to have a question on citizenship—Is this person a citizen of the United States?—when you're counting up population and other related data. Unless the reason behind the question was not innocent. Unless it was a smoke screen for another motive.

The supposed rationale for the question was based on a letter signed in late 2017 by Arthur Gary, career lawyer at the Justice Department, to Commerce Department officials stating: "The Department of Justice is committed to robust and even-handed enforcement of the Nation's civil rights laws and fair elections for all Americans. In furtherance of that commitment, I write on behalf of the Department to formally request that the Census Bureau reinstate on the 2020 Census questionnaire a question regarding citizenship, formerly included in the so-called 'long form' census. This data is critical to the Department's enforcement of Section 2 of the Voting Rights Act and its important protections against racial discrimination in voting." There was nothing innocent about it. It was the opposite of innocent.

The scheme—and it turned out to be a scheme—to add a question about citizenship was nothing but an attempt to undermine the Voting Rights Act. Instead of assuring people's right to vote, it would intimidate people into *not* being counted, scare them into *not* voting, thereby limiting their power, rights, and benefits. The Voting Rights Act is not just another law to me. It is sacred. And it has been, to me and every person of color, since the day of its inspiration in 1957.

I was eight years old in 1957, a little kid. But I was old enough to know that besides my parents, the most significant figure in my life and in the lives of all black people was Dr. Martin Luther King. When he spoke, we heard him. On the radio, on television, in the newspapers, at rallies. He was our guiding light. I was only eight in 1957, but when Dr. King gave one of his most historic speeches, and he implored, exhorted, demanded, "Give us the ballot," I knew it was a moment in time we would not forget. Those were four powerful words—"Give us the ballot"— because the ballot, that is, votes are the most powerful weapon in a democracy. Votes can change history. Votes can change who is in office, where we can live, where we can go to school, how much we can earn, who we can marry . . . life itself.

But didn't we get the vote after the Civil War? The Fifteenth

Amendment to the Constitution, passed in 1870, states: "The right of citizens of the United States to vote shall not be denied or abridged by the United States or by any State on account of race, color, or previous condition of servitude." Why did we need to demand the vote all over again? Because during Reconstruction, the vote had systematically been denied or taken away by law and/or intimidation. Jim Crow laws, legalizing segregation, and passed state by state, allowed those states to discriminate on the basis of poll taxes, literacy tests, and other arbitrary restrictions. And by the way, the Fifteenth Amendment only applied to men, not women. That wouldn't come until 1920 and the Nineteenth Amendment.

Still, it wasn't until almost a hundred years after black men supposedly got the vote, almost fifty years after women got the vote, and almost a decade after King's speech, on August 6, 1965, that the Voting Rights Act was finally passed. It was nearly a century between the promise and the reality. There is a photograph that I can still picture of President Lyndon Johnson handing the pen with which he signed the act to Martin Luther King, the man who would not rest until it became law.

In January 2019, I worked on a bill called the For the People Act—a reaffirmation and extension of voting rights, including campaign finance reform, ethics provisions requiring disclosure of candidate tax returns, a national voting day, prevention of gerrymandering, and prohibitions on voter roll purging. It passed the House but is blocked in the Senate so far. We will keep fighting for it. If we must pass voting rights legislation over and over, so be it. If we have to protect and ensure our vote over and over, so be it.

To this day, and especially on this day in Congress, I recall Dr. King's words from 1957—"Give us the ballot." I can see him and hear him. Truth be told, I don't know if I remember King's speech from listening to it on the radio, or watching it on television, or from my mother and father talking about it at the dinner table, or from just hearing the story told over and over through the years, but those words have never left me. Give us the ballot. And that means you cannot have my ballot. My ballot is not for sale. It is my right.

So when the president or his foot soldiers attempt to intimidate me or others, to dilute that ballot, or restrict it, or find a way to reinvent Jim Crow laws, I will not be silent.

That is why we held a hearing—to protect the right to vote, not to threaten it. That's why we asked the secretary of commerce, Wilbur Ross, whose department was leading the 2020 census efforts, to testify under oath.

My opening statement laid out the situation in no uncertain terms: "Today we will [also] examine Secretary Ross' decision to add a new citizenship question after experts—listen up—at the Census Bureau warned, and I quote, that 'it harms the quality of the census count.' Let that sink in. The very organization Ross claimed to be aiding, the Census Bureau, issued a caution that the new question 'harms the quality' of their count. And that's what they do, count."

I went on to state what was becoming obvious: the dubiousness of Ross's credibility, and the credibility of the administration's claimed motives. "We have serious questions about whether Secretary Ross was truthful when he appeared before Congress last year and testified on three occasions that he added the citizenship question only because the Department of Justice requested it. [March 20 and 22, and May 10, 2018] . . . New documents showed that he was engaged in a secret campaign to add the citizenship question from the very first days after he arrived at the Department of Commerce. . . . He became impatient when his demands were not being met and he was working with officials at the highest levels of the Trump Administration . . . including Steve Bannon and Jeff Sessions. These are facts. They are not in dispute. Two judges—two judges—have already struck down the citizenship question, . . . that Secretary Ross 'violated federal law and the United States Constitution.' And they found that his claim of merely responding to a request from the Department of Justice was a pretext and a false one. Again, I didn't say that, the judges said that. . . . The Trump Administration . . . claimed that adding the citizenship question was necessary to obtain better data to enforce the Voting Rights Act. . . . I don't know anyone who truly believes that the Trump Administration is interested in enhancing the Voting Rights Act. [This drew some low laughter from the members, I suspect even some Republicans.] This Administration has done everything in its power to suppress the vote, not to help people exercise their right to vote. . . . I have championed voting rights all of my adult life. . . . In the more than 50 years . . . the Voting Rights Act enforcement has never used citizenship data from every household. . . . The judges . . . held that the Voting Rights Act claim was a fake justification for the citizenship question. I didn't say it. They said it. One judge ruled . . . that Secretary Ross . . . 'concealed its true basis rather than explaining it.' So the key question we will ask Secretary Ross today is, *what was he hiding from Congress?* What's the real reason that the Trump Administration wanted to add this unconstitutional citizenship question?"

We, and the whole country, eventually learned the real reason. Thanks to our hearing and further investigation, we found out what was behind the citizenship question: suppressing, not ensuring the vote. Noncitizens, that is immigrants, faced with such a question, would be afraid to identify themselves, afraid to be counted, and those lower counts would enable redistricting—gerrymandering—to favor Republicans. An added plus for conservative lawmakers was that lower counts would deny billions of dollars of federal aid for critical services to areas based on lower population counts. The true story unfolded like a bad television plot. The sad part was, it wasn't a TV show. It was truth. A documentary of truth.

When asked for justification of his support of the citizenship question, Wilbur Ross, not surprisingly, cited the Justice Department letter on the Voting Rights Act. We asked Ross if he expected us to believe the Trump administration was suddenly the protector of voting rights. We asked if we were supposed to buy the argument that it was the real reason behind the citizenship question. We asked about the origin and author(s) of the letter. The letter had supposedly been written by Arthur Gary, counsel at Justice. Had Commerce or Ross requested a letter? Who else was involved? He refused to answer some questions. He answered other questions with party-line rhetoric. He wouldn't cooperate. But we kept at it. And so did the media. Little by little the truth came out. It turns out the letter was not the sole work of Gary; it was the brainchild of a gerrymandering expert,

Thomas Hofeller, who had come up with a complex scheme of suppressing the population count to lessen the voting strength of brown and black communities, in an effort to maximize Republican political power and minimize Democratic representation in subsequent elections.

We kept asking. The media kept digging. Hofeller's work coincided with the work of White House redistricting advocate Kris Kobach, whose unsupported political stances have included: the Obama birther movement, illegal voters accounted for Hillary Clinton's popular majority, and immigrants commit more crimes than non-immigrants. We interviewed John Gore, a Department of Justice attorney, and learned that census advisor Mark Neuman, a longtime friend of Hofeller, who helped create the framework for a letter, sent it on to Gore, who actually wrote the letter, and then passed it on to another Justice attorney, Arthur Gary. Gary did not write the letter! A good soldier, he just signed it. And the letter asserting that citizenship count was needed to enforce the Voting Rights Act was sent to Commerce as their rationale. It was never about the Voting Rights Act. Not for one minute. They might have gotten away with that if not for one little thing. Hofeller died. His daughter, who it turns out wasn't on such good terms with him, found his computer hard drive records and uncovered his relationship with the Trump administration and their efforts to use citizenship as a smoke screen for redistricting. She turned the drives over to a team working on a related case of gerrymandering in North Carolina and that's when the evidence came to light. That light sparked a fire. And the Voting Rights Act enforcement fiction went up in smoke. Ross had set out to add the citizenship question from the time he took office as secretary and he engineered the Department of Justice involvement as pretext. Remember that word, "pretext": a reason given that is not the real reason.

That wasn't just the committee's opinion. That's what the Supreme Court said. In June, in a 5–4 decision, Chief Justice John Roberts upheld the lower court rulings stating that Secretary Ross's claim of enforcing the Voting Rights Act "appears to be contrived." He spelled out the flaws, contradictions, and outright lies in their flimsy case. Among other quotes from the decision: "The secretary . . . was determined to reinstate a citizenship question from the time he entered office; instructed his staff to make it happen; waited while commerce officials explored whether another agency would request census-based citizenship data; subsequently contacted the attorney general himself to ask if D.O.J. would make the request; and adopted the Voting Rights Act rationale late in the process."

They (the justices) "cannot ignore the disconnect between the decision made and the explanation given" [by the lawyers for the Trump administration]. "Accepting contrived reasons would defeat the purpose of the enterprise. If judicial review is to be more than an empty ritual, it must demand something better than the explanation offered for the action taken in this case. . . . Altogether, the evidence tells a story that does not match the explanation the secretary gave for his decision."

From a legal standpoint, that decision didn't totally close the door on the citizenship question. It said the reason Commerce had given for it was invalid. That meant they could try to find another reason and fight it. But given the circumstances, they would be contradicting their own original argument. *We said the reason was X. Oh, no, we meant Y.* It would mean admitting that they had fabricated their reasoning. And Commerce had claimed they needed a fast decision from the Court in order to make the deadline to print the census. If that was real, they had to go to press. After some posturing that they would keep fighting for the question, they folded.

It was a win. That's why oversight is critical. That's why freedom of the press is critical. That's democracy. We didn't have too many outright victories but this was one. At least for now. I felt like I had kept a promise to my mother.

My mother on her dying bed, at ninety-two years old, uttered some words to me that I shall never forget, that are part of my DNA. She was lying on her deathbed and didn't say, "Elijah, I love you." She did not say, "Elijah, I'm proud of you." The very last words that she spoke before she died were, "Do not let anyone take our votes away." Martin Luther King said, "Give us the ballot." My mother, Ruth Cummings, said, "Do not let anyone take our votes away." And I heed the words of both of them.

WE FOLLOWED THE census hearing with the first of many more on the administration's blatant lack of transparency, withholding records and documents, and defying subpoenas. We asked. They said no. We ordered. They said no. We subpoenaed. They said no. That was their strategy—no. Over and over and over, the White House stalled; they tried to discredit not only our committee's investigations, but the work of the Judicial, Intelligence, and Finance Committees of the House as well. Why? If you have nothing to hide, open up, show up, speak up.

If you're not doing anything wrong, you have nothing to worry about. Yet they obstructed. They stalled. They blocked. Why?

I have been in Congress for two decades and I have seen partisan battles. I've seen bitter fights. Ugly words. But I had never, never in twelve terms in the House of Representatives seen this kind of unapologetic, unrepentant, stonewalled, refusal to see, hear, speak, or deal with, or even acknowledge reality. I have seen the opposite. I have seen gestures of honesty, of courage, of conscience, of what is right. I had witnessed the highly divisive Clinton impeachment, when some House Democrats crossed party lines and voted to impeach because they thought the president's behavior was wrong, and some Senate Republicans voted to acquit because they did not find his actions worthy of removal from office. I had seen John McCain, dying of brain cancer, bravely cast a vote against the abolition of Obamacare because he believed it would simply be wrong. I had seen Democrats and Republicans cooperate on budget bills, on defense, on homeland security after 9/11, on financial recovery measures after the crash of 2008. I had seen members of Congress, no matter their politics, live up to their oaths of office, choose loyalty to country over party, to honor the Constitution, to act as the check and balance of the executive branch. I had never seen anything like what we were witnessing. A denial of duty and reality. Why? Why? Why?

A LITTLE BEFORE 10 a.m., on Wednesday, May 22, 2019, I made my way from my office in the Rayburn Building to the Congressional Auditorium in the Capitol Visitors Center—it was the weekly Democratic caucus. The 450-seat, theater-style room was pretty well packed with my colleagues and their staff. Every Democratic representative in the House is a member of the caucus. In "normal times," whatever those were, attendance could be spotty, not mandatory, and we all have more work than time. But these days, if House Speaker Pelosi says it's important to be there, you're there.

From January 3, the very first day of the 116th Congress, to the day of this meeting, the Trump White House had stonewalled our congressional work at every turn, refusing to turn over documents, openly urging witnesses to be uncooperative and flaunt subpoenas, invoking "executive privilege" where there was no privilege to invoke, making threats or dangling pardons, and subverting the constitutional balance of power. Today, Speaker Pelosi asked all members to try their best to attend and in particular urged the committee chairs.

The meeting was called to order by the caucus chair, Hakeem Jeffries of New York, and he then turned it over to the Speaker. She asked for updates on each committee's investigations—each one was carrying out critical, historic work; the work of each was being flagrantly defied by the White House—Judicial, Intelligence, Oversight, Ways and Means, and more. Jerry Nadler, Judiciary chair, led off, detailing his committee's planned hearings and the obstacles being thrown in their way. As Oversight chair, I went next, listing our work and a similar litany of White House roadblocks. There were murmurs, and uh-huhs and head nods. We all knew that every committee report would echo the others—delays, denials, and dodges, blockades, barriers, and brick walls. I interrupted the reports. I had something to say to the entire caucus. We knew the truth we were facing. I held up my hand asking for silence. Then I spoke and called out that truth. "If you don't remember any other word from today, you must add this word to your vocabulary; that word is 'cover-up.'" I repeated it. "Cover-up. If there is one word you should take out of this meeting, that is it." I knew that my message hit home. You could feel it in the room. Cover-up rang true. Too true.

We did go through the committee reports and they did echo each other. Then, not surprisingly, the topic turned to impeachment. As a body led by the Speaker, we had decided we should proceed with our investigations—the preparatory work for an impeachment inquiry—but not vote on formal articles of impeachment. Not yet.

We had determined that, despite all the tactics to hinder us, we could learn more and accomplish more this way, through relentless investigations, and through the courts and court decisions, than with formal impeachment proceedings. At this moment in time, impeachment seemed to be doomed to end with a nonconviction in the Republican-controlled Senate. Yes, among some in the party, the tide for impeachment was strong and not subsiding, but Speaker Pelosi was equally resolute. She knew, as we all did, that the day might well arrive when it would be time to invoke the articles of impeachment, and so it was important to be as prepared as possible. We wanted every shred of evidence. We wanted a case that would be hard, if not impossible to deny. If the Senate held a trial and ultimately did not convict for political reasons, we wanted the public, the country, and the world to see the case and judge for themselves. So we continued our work. We continued to press for information, records, documents, facts, evidence.

After an hour and a half, the meeting was adjourned and we left the room to face the press outside the doors—always waiting for the word or line or phrase that might be the day's sound bite. They got what they wanted.

Nancy Pelosi faced the microphones and cameras and said, "We believe that no one is above the law, including the president of the United States. And we believe the president of the United States is engaged in a [pause] cover-up."

Then another House member used the word "cover-up," and then another. Within minutes, and repeatedly, you heard "cover-up . . . cover-up . . . cover-up" on CNN, MSNBC, NBC, ABC, CBS, Fox News, on talk radio and read it in *Politico*, *Roll Call*, *The Hill*, on social media, everywhere.

"Cover-up" quickly got to the president and got under his skin. Furious, he came out to the Rose Garden and said, "I don't do cover-ups." He slammed the Democrats in Congress for pursuing investigations into his financial dealings, his businesses, and his entire administration. He canceled his scheduled meeting with Speaker Pelosi on infrastructure. His sound bite—"I don't do cover-ups"—was played and/or quoted over the next hours and days as well. Some network commentators even listed the numerous and obvious cover-ups he said he does not do.

"Cover-up" is strong stuff. It isn't just saying your opponent is on the other side from you; that's to be expected, even respected. No, it's saying he or she is hiding something. Or maybe lots of things. Documents. Transcripts. Witnesses. Deeds. Actions. Smoking guns. And doing it with a plan. A concerted, relentless, dark plan to prevent the truth from being seen or heard.

I didn't get to that place easily. It's not my nature or my instinct or in my heart. I don't look for conspiracies or plots. I look for allies and common ground. That's the way I was raised and that's the way I serve. That carried me through my years in the Maryland General Assembly and then my twelve consecutive terms in the U.S. Congress. I've faced challenge after challenge—Republican presidents Reagan and George H. W. Bush, the Clinton impeachment, the dead-heat Bush-Gore election decided on party lines by the Supreme Court, the bare-knuckle politics of House Speaker Newt Gingrich, the rise of the Tea Party and the Freedom Caucus, the anti-Obama birthers, Hillary Clinton's stunning loss. But I had never faced obstruction. Bald-faced, unapologetic refusal to play by the rules. I had never faced Donald Trump or his tactics. Nor have my colleagues. Nor have the American people.

That's what led me to say to the Democratic caucus, this is a "cover-up." I will live by my values, by what my parents taught me, but I, and we as a country, will meet this challenge. As I often say, *Do not mistake my kindness for weakness.* I am the chairman of the House Committee on Oversight and Reform. If ever, ever in the history of this country, we have been in need of oversight and reform, it is now.

ON JULY 12 and July 18, 2019, we had scheduled hearings on the immigration situation—the child separation policy—and conditions at the Texas-Mexico border, with Acting Secretary of Homeland Security Kevin McAleenan. The policy that literally dismantled families at the border had supposedly been implemented in April 2018. But it turned out the practice, without the authority, had begun a year earlier. Parents were taken to court and prosecuted while their children were herded into mass, inhumane warehousing facilities, neglected, underfed, under-cared for, treated like animals. I knew I had to conduct a fair and unbiased hearing but when I learned of the abuses, I was sickened and could barely contain my outrage. I have dealt with bad things in my life and career. Crime. Violence. Death. I can deal with the realities of wrongdoing. But to abuse children is something I cannot stomach.

Still, as chair of the committee, I vowed to carry out the hearing properly and thoroughly. Still, my committee members would prep on the issues, investigate, and then question the secretary. Still, we would seek and find the truth. My committee included savvy, experienced legislators as well as new, young, determined, idealistic members of the so-called Squad. Who are they?

When I took over as chair and it was time to put new members on the committee, I said to Nancy Pelosi, "give me freshmen." I have twenty-two members, plus myself. Five are in their first terms and three more are only in their second. That's a lot of young folks. But I love the enthusiasm and energy of young members. I love the opportunity to mentor, and I love to learn from them as much as I teach them. On the committee I have freshmen Alexandria Ocasio-Cortez, Rashida Tlaib, Ayanna Pressley, Katie Hill, and Harley Rouda—a Hispanic Latina from New York, a Muslim from Michigan, an African-American from Massachusetts, a millennial from California, and an older first-termer and Republican turned Democrat—bold, smart, fearless people, leaders for tomorrow, from backgrounds that haven't typically been well represented in the government. I can relate. Three of the five women, Ocasio-Cortez, Tlaib, and Pressley, along with Ilhan Omar of Minnesota (not a member of the committee), have earned the nickname "the Squad," for their outspoken voices and refusal to be quiet "kids." I love the Squad. I love their passion for their work.

And if ever there was a job for young, outspoken, idealistic crusaders—aka the Squad—this was it. A few weeks before the hearing, Alexandria Ocasio-Cortez, or AOC as she's become known, had come to me and said she and her colleagues wanted to visit the border to witness the immigrant detention facilities firsthand, in preparation for the hearings. I was all for it. But I'd told her that our committee couldn't and shouldn't fund their trip. I told her to have her own office and the offices of the other members pay for the trip, and that way their work and reports would never be subject to accusations that the committee sent them on a mission to gain damning evidence for the hearings.

They did use their own budgets; they went; they reported from the border and they brought firsthand accounts of horrific treatment back to Congress and the country. AOC tweeted from the border, "Now I've seen the inside of these facilities. It's not just the kids. It's everyone. People drinking out of toilets, officers laughing in front of members of Congress. I brought it up to their superiors. They said 'officers are under stress & act out sometimes.' No accountability." She sent pictures of people living on small blankets, sharing food, being mocked and treated with disdain by the Border Patrol, the very people supposedly looking out for them.

Tlaib tweeted, "We can't just focus on the children anymore.

I met grandmothers, mothers and fathers who are suffering. This is devastating. The look in one father's eyes broke me. I can't look away." After the tour, she said, "It is my duty as a congresswoman, and an American, to raise hell until immigrants seeking safety and a better life are treated with dignity, respect, and see their human rights protected."

Joe Kennedy III, also visiting the border, sent his own tweet: "Do not miss the racist, sexist slurs @RashidaTlaib @RepEscobar @AOC @AyannaPressley and others face for doing their jobs. Nor the fact that they continue to fight like hell anyways."

Before the tour began, Pressley had stated, "I [am] committed . . . to addressing these human rights violations . . . to getting these children and their families out of incarceration." Afterward she added, "This is about the preservation of our humanity . . . about seeing every single person there as a member of your own family. I am tired of the health and the safety, the humanity and the full freedoms of black and brown children being negotiated and compromised and moderated."

After the tour, at a press conference the congresswomen held, protesters and mobs shouted racist, sexist, vile epithets at them. Tlaib and Omar faced one loud voice shouting, "We don't want Muslims here." The crowd should have been applauding their bravery and dedication to freedom and democracy, not attacking their heritage. The crowd should have been looking inward because every single one of them, without exception, comes from ancestors who came from somewhere else, who came here for a better life, not to be locked up at the border and made to drink from toilets.

The first hearing focused on the child separation policy.

Texas Democrat Veronica Escobar, Alexandria Ocasio-Cortez, Ayanna Pressley, and Rashida Tlaib testified as witnesses, having been to the border and seen the horrific conditions there. Additionally, we had expert testimony from Jennifer Costello, acting inspector general of the Department of Homeland Security; Thomas Homan, former acting director, Immigration and Customs Enforcement; Ann Maxwell, assistant inspector general for evaluation and inspections, Department of Health and Human Services; Elora Mukherjee, director of Immigrants' Rights Clinic, Columbia Law School; and Jennifer Nagda, policy director, Young Center for Immigrant Children's Rights. The experts restated and reinforced the standards that should be met, that were being ignored or flaunted.

From the members of Congress who visited the southern border, we heard chilling accounts of children—five, six, seven, ten, and twelve years old—torn away from their parents, living in cages—often two, three, or more to a cage—with no toilet facilities, no soap, wearing the same clothing day after day. They recounted stories of the mothers, warehoused in detention centers, living on six-foot-square pads with aluminum blankets, enduring insults from guards, wondering, worrying, crying over the whereabouts and well-being of their estranged children. Since the crackdowns at the border had begun in 2017 and 2018, at least 2,800 children had been separated from their parents. Efforts were supposedly being made to reunite families. But the Trump administration acknowledged that in 2019, at least seven hundred more had been separated. It was disgraceful. It was disgusting. It was inexcusable. It was almost impossible to hear.

I confess, I turned my head several times and retreated into my own thoughts. I thought about the Statue of Liberty and the words inscribed: "Give me your tired, your poor, your huddled masses yearning to breathe free. . . ." Lady Liberty would be turning her head, too. But I also had thoughts closer to home, a memory of my father one Christmas.

When I was growing up, some years were better than others, and some not so good at all. In good years my parents would manage to scrape together money to buy us kids nice gifts, but there were other years when they couldn't. One of those not-so-good years was when W. R. Grace Chemical Company, where my father worked, was on strike. He even told us in advance not to expect much in the way of gifts from Santa. As children, we thought, how could Santa let us down? We just didn't want to believe it. But on Christmas morning, when all of us kids came into the living room, we didn't see any wrapped packages. Not one. Any hopes of skates or games or baseball bats or puzzles were gone.

My father sat in his favorite chair and watched us, with a sad look on his face. My mother sat next to him, with the same sad expression. We looked up at daddy and in his hands were toothbrushes, one for each of us. Toothbrushes? They probably cost a dollar or less apiece. Naturally, being kids, we couldn't help but be disappointed and I guess our faces showed it. But he didn't allow us to be disappointed. He explained again that this was a difficult time for our family, but it was still Christmas.

After giving each of us our toothbrush, he said to all of us, "You will not understand this now, but you will understand it by and by. My presence in your life is presents enough."

My presence in your life is presents enough.

He was speaking not only for himself, but for my mother, too. Parents being there, in body and in spirit, was the greatest gift a child could have. You can't wrap that up and put a bow on it. You may not appreciate it on Christmas but you can appreciate it in your life. Lots of kids had one parent or none, didn't even know their daddy or their mom, were raised by aunts or grandmothers or neighbors or the state. The toothbrush was a symbol, a token, something small that was needed. But our parents being there with us, that was the real gift.

I thought about that story in the middle of the testimony on the child separation policy. No child, not one single child anywhere on this earth, should ever, ever be separated from his or her loving mother or father. It is wrong. Just plain wrong. But that's what we, the United States of America, were doing at our own borders. That's not a policy. It's a sin, a shameful sin.

I had to turn back to the business of the hearings. I had to prepare for the second hearing. But the image of my father and his words stayed in my mind.

BETWEEN THE TWO hearings, there were rumblings of a "family squabble" between the Squad members and Speaker Pelosi. The rumor was that the Speaker thought the young lawmakers were somewhat undisciplined in their rhetoric, and that they, in turn, thought she was trying to muffle them. In fact, neither was the case. Yes, they do speak their minds, individually and with conscience, and at the same time, Nancy has the job of getting the House majority to speak with one voice.

Quietly, I spoke to Nancy and said, "We have to embrace

these new folks. They are our future." She agreed and had already reached out to them; they were all on the same page.

Of course, Trump tried to exploit the moment to denigrate the young lawmakers. He went on a classic Trump tweet rampage. "So interesting to see 'Progressive' Democrat Congresswomen, who originally came from countries whose governments are a complete and total catastrophe, the worst, most corrupt and inept anywhere in the world, now loudly and viciously telling the people of the United States, the greatest and most powerful Nation on earth, how our government is to be run. Why don't they go back and help fix the totally broken and crime infested places from which they came. Then come back and show us how it is done. These places need your help badly, you can't leave fast enough. I'm sure that Nancy Pelosi would be very happy to quickly work out free travel arrangements!"

As usual, in the middle of his rant, he didn't even have his facts right. Only one of the congresswomen was born outside the United States, but the president was stoking nationalism, Islamophobia, sexism, racism, any "ism" or "phobia" he could use to fire up his base and divide the country. At one of Trump's subsequent rallies in North Carolina, he launched into the attack again and the crowd took the bait and chanted, "Send her back."

But instead of dividing the Democrats, he united us. Everyone called it what it was. Hate. Turning Americans against Americans.

In the second hearing, we had Acting Secretary of Homeland Security Kevin McAleenan under oath and accountable. He had to respond directly to the eyewitness reports, and to me confronting his department and his own personal values. The department had what they call a "zero tolerance" policy, put in place in April 2018 by then–attorney general Jeff Sessions. Think about those words—"zero tolerance." What that meant was that no one who is technically illegal or undocumented may enter the country and that in the process of enforcing the policy, children may be separated from parents, no matter the age, illness, or frailty of a child, no matter how far a family has traveled, no matter the political situation they are fleeing, no matter what. Infants can be taken from a nursing mother. Think about that. Zero tolerance. Not strict enforcement, or rigid or firm enforcement, but total and absolute, without allowing for specific conditions or details, no exceptions. None. How could one human being treat other human beings like that?

I tried to conduct my questions calmly and evenly: "We hear about stories coming out from you and your agency that everything is pretty good, that you're doing a great job. I guess you feel like you're doing a great job. Right?" He began to answer, "We're doing our level best in a challenging—" But I could not control my outrage and cut in, "What does that mean? What does that mean when a child is sitting in their own feces, can't take a shower? Come on, man. What is that about? None of us would have our children in that position. They are human beings. . . . I've said it before and I'll say it again, 'It is not the deed you do to a child. It's the memory.' It's the memory. . . . We are the United States of America. We are the greatest country in the world. We are the ones that can go anywhere . . . and save people, make sure they have diapers, make sure they have toothbrushes, make sure they're not laying around defecating on some . . . paper. Come on. We're better than that. . . ."

My voice rose, my face heated, my fists clenched, I looked up to God. I have tried mightily over my career to be a man of calm in a storm, to look for common, or at least not rocky ground between people. Sometimes I have had to fight my inner instincts to do it. Sometimes I fail. That day, at that moment, I vowed, despite my indignation, to cling to my calm. It was all I could do. I looked down. I paused. I moved on.

I expressed my concern that he or the administration simply did not feel for other humans. I wondered if they lacked the most basic instinct of sharing the emotions—the pain—of other people. Did they have an "empathy deficit"?

But the secretary had so little to say, so little in the way of answers. There are no answers to questions of a lack of humanity. To an empathy deficit. I don't even think it was all his fault. They put him in that situation—the White House, the administration, and his own department. They didn't give him the money or the people to do what had to be done. The administration had provided a godless response.

It reminded me of Hurricane Katrina. Was the horrible performance in the face of the hurricane's brutal damage the fault of the Federal Emergency Management Agency (FEMA), of the staff and leadership . . . or the fault of President George W. Bush? President Bush did not authorize enough help. President Bush did not send in enough aid, enough money, enough supplies soon enough, before the conditions got so dire. At that time, I said at a news conference, "God would not be pleased with our response." I said it again after Trump's pathetic reaction to Hurricane Maria and the devastating destruction in Puerto Rico. President Trump acted like it wasn't his responsibility. He acted like the havoc and ruin, the power losses, the food shortages, and the water contamination, all the suffering just wasn't that bad. Or that the U.S. action, or inaction, was acceptable. No, God was not pleased again. Now, at our borders, with children in cages, sleeping in feces, torn from their mothers—God was surely not pleased. God was angry. The president of the United States and the White House kept upping the ante, kept ratcheting up the tough talk, on arrests and raids, and let the onus and blame fall on his people, the Department of Homeland Security.

Still, as acting head of the department, it was McAleenan's job to answer. His answers, or his lack of answers, were not acceptable. Not acceptable to decency. What he was accountable for, no doubt, was the behavior of his own people, the Border Patrol. That included not only how they were treating children, mothers, fathers, and grandparents, but their own language, attitude, and acts toward us, the U.S. public and their representatives in government, the people looking out for the welfare of these children and families, the people he and his staff actually work for.

Representative Ocasio-Cortez questioned him on the actions and attitudes of his staff and what was being done about it: "Did you see the posts mocking migrant children's deaths?"

He responded with obvious discomfort, "I did."

She continued, "Did you see the posts planning physical harm to myself and Congresswoman Escobar?"

He offered a defense: "Yes, and I directed an investigation within minutes of reading the article."

She would not let up. "Did you see the images of officers circulating photoshopped images of my violent rape?"

Again, he had to acknowledge the ugly facts: "Yes, I did."

She then asked the critical question, about whether he had taken the action he had the power to take, to remove the offenders from their positions: "Are those officers on the job today and responsible for the safety of migrant women and children?"

He reverted to bureaucracy-speak: "[T]here is an aggressive investigation on this issue proceeding. You've heard the chief of the Border Patrol, the most senior female official in law enforcement across the entire country, say that these posts do not meet our standards of conduct, and they will be followed up aggressively."

Ocasio-Cortez asked again, pushing for a straight yes or no answer—are these people still on the job? The secretary responded: "We've already put individuals on administrative duties. I don't know which ones correspond with which posts. And we've issued cease and desist orders to dozens more."

There was one moment in the hearings I actually saw as a good sign—small, but still a sign nonetheless. When pressed on whether separating children and families fosters a "dehumanizing culture" in his department, the secretary adamantly defended the organization. "We do not have a dehumanizing culture at CBP . . . [The department] rescues 4,000 people a year" and is "absolutely committed to the well-being of everyone that they interact with." That answer offered a glimmer of morality and conscience in McAleenan's view of his job. He recognized the department's role was *meant* to protect the "well-being" of people. Even if they were failing to carry it out, even if they were crippled by inadequate budgets and manpower, even if they were poisoned by ugly rhetoric—the empathy deficit—from the top of the Trump administration. Do I forgive him?

No. It is not enough to know right from wrong. You cannot just stand by and watch wrong go on. But, in his heart, I don't believe Kevin McAleenan is a bad man. He seems to be an individual who knows what his department is *supposed* to do. He may be presiding over inhumane acts but he does not seem to condone them. His sin is that he has not acted. But personally, I was not surprised when a few weeks later, he resigned his position. Do I forgive him? No. I separate his unacceptable behavior from what may be his conscience. I see him almost as two people. One bad. One maybe redeemable.

How can I do that? Why do I do it? I was taught by my parents, by the church, not to demonize people, even if they had committed a bad deed, but rather to allow for redemption. Sometimes that is very hard to do, to forgive or allow for the possibility of forgiveness, but I try. I remind myself that we are all flawed. A few years ago, Maya and I heard Bryan Stevenson, founder of the Equal Justice Initiative—fighting for prisoners on death row—speak in Washington D.C. and Stevenson's words stayed with me: "Each of us is better than the worst thing we have done." I believe that. I try very hard to practice that belief.

And I do something else. Something that is sometimes good, sometimes not so good. I compartmentalize. I separate people and actions sometimes from their deeds, sometimes from each other. An important person in one part of my life may not know of another important person in another part of my life. I have done this for almost my whole life. My daughters, Jennifer and Adia, recognize it. My friends and professional colleagues are aware I do it. My wife, Maya, knows it well and has called me on it. Good or bad, it helps me navigate rough waters or challenging individuals. But I realize it can also create barriers. I compart-mentalize. It helps me keep my emotions in the right place. I hope sometimes that other folks will do the same for me. I can get cranky—so I've been told—but when it's over, it's over, dealt with, finished.

But above all, I have special relationships—the good side of compartments. I put family first and always. I have strong ties to my longtime staffers. I connect with Democrats and with some Republicans. I have a place in my heart for my first legal partner, campaign advisor, and all-around confidant, Mike Christianson. I have a bond—a true bond—with Maya. I share my day's work each night with her and sort out how to take on the next day. Each is a compartment, a special compartment. I don't have a lot of friends, but those I have, I have for life. I tell my daughters, "You've got to keep your friends. You don't want to ever be alone." People at work may change sides or aims or leave. But friends, real friends, and that includes family members that are real friends, they are there forever, if you take care of them.

Maybe I compartmentalize too much. Maybe I should share more with more people. Maybe I find or hope for good in the Kevin McAleenans of the world when I shouldn't. But my most sacred relationship is with God and he teaches us that forgive-ness and understanding make up an important compartment.

Truth be told, I have not found a compartment for the presi-dent, at least not one that is merciful.

THE WEEKEND AFTER the second hearing, I appeared on *This Week* with George Stephanopoulos. On the show, I uttered words it truly hurt me to say. After the vile attacks by Trump on the young congresswomen, George asked me, "Do you believe President Trump is a racist?"

I didn't answer quickly. I paused, I thought, I prayed. And then I told the truth.

"Yes, no doubt about it." I said, "I tried to give him the benefit of the doubt." But there was no more benefit to give him. There was no more doubt. His behavior, his language, his anger, his hate all led to only one conclusion. Unfortunately, I know that behavior, language, anger, and hate all too well. I've seen it, heard it, and felt it many times in my life. I felt it as a child walking through a white neighborhood for the chance to swim in a pool. I felt it when my father came home from work, doing the "colored jobs." I felt it when my mother took the bus home from cleaning the fancy homes north of us. I felt it when black law students were only admitted to the bar in limited quotas simply because they were black. I felt it when police arrested young black men at double or triple the rate of white men. I felt it when Freddie Gray was killed. I felt it with every funeral I attended. I felt it when I saw mortgages foreclosed. I felt it when I drove my car through a white suburb. I felt it when I heard names called. And frankly, I felt it when it was unspoken but equally loud.

Those were difficult weeks for the nation, and for me personally. The two issues—the citizenship question and cruelty to immigrants—were really one issue—the treatment of human beings, and that hit home to me.

As a black American, my ancestors were not immigrants, that is, people seeking freedom in new lands. On the contrary, they were free, then they were enslaved and forcibly brought to America.

I am the son of sharecroppers, the grandson of African-descended people held as slaves. They did not come here for a better life. They were kidnapped, put in chains, auctioned off, kept in bondage, working not for wages but just to stay alive. But they were, in some sense, refugees, defined as "persons who have been forced to leave their country," though usually refugees had to leave to escape war or other disaster. Instead, my ancestors were made to leave their countries by force.

Years later, after we were finally, technically freed, many of us did become what might be called immigrants by leaving southern states and coming north for what we thought might be a better life, better jobs, better situations for our children, more freedom to participate in the American dream. We were asylum seekers like the Irish, Italians, and Jews before us, and the families now flocking to our borders from Guatemala, Honduras, and Mexico. We wanted to preserve our culture and customs—not the culture of slave owners, but our culture, our history, our roots. We wanted to raise families without fear. We wanted to practice our religion. Speak our language. Revere our heritage. In freedom. We came north with hope.

These past several weeks and months have been a direct assault on that hope. The census question would have literally scared off, cut out, and denied benefits and the vote to thousands of people—black, white, and brown—as disenfranchised as during slavery. The border crackdown and treatment were equally egregious, equally reminiscent of the slave trade days when family separation was common. My ancestors were taken from parents in African villages, marched to slave ships, chained in the galleys, barely fed, forced to lie in their own excrement, and then sold off to plantation owners. Any families they managed to form were subject to being broken up, with children, husbands, and wives sold to the highest bidder. How much different was that than having young children separated from mothers and fathers, put into cages, denied soap or water, sleeping in their own excrement, fed rations, verbally abused, and mocked? Where is the dream of freedom? What happened to the prospect of a better life? Why was our nation turning its back on its promise?

This hurt all of us. It hurt me deeply and personally. I could hear and see my parents and my grandparents weeping in heaven. I witnessed my own children's anxiety. I felt my neighbors' and constituents' outright fear. This was not America.

I recalled a chance occurrence, a small moment, that I experienced a long time ago. It had hit me so hard and so deeply, I wrote about it for a newspaper story in 2008, and it stayed with me ever since, but almost haunted me on the days of the hearings.

SHARING THE HEART OF A STRANGER

Last Saturday began as an ordinary day for me—the Saturday before Mother's Day. That afternoon, returning home from buying some flowers for the occasion . . .

As I drove into the filling station, I was startled to see a young man lying on the pavement, struggling to get up. Again and again, he would try to rise—but each time, he would fall back.

In horror, I realized that blood was gushing from his chest with each attempt. . . . I jumped from my car and kneeled by the young man's side to see if I could help him. . . . I held the stranger's head in one arm while I tried to apply pressure to where the blood was spurting. I told him to remain calm—that I would wait with him until an ambulance arrived. . . .

After a few moments, I realized that his cries to me were in Spanish. He did not understand what I was trying to say to him. . . . I fumbled in my pocket, found my cell phone, and dialed [my wife, Maya] who speaks Spanish. . . ."How do you say, 'It's going to be all right'?"

The young man kept gasping for air. It took my own breath away, and I struggled not to faint. . . . We may have begun as strangers, but we were trapped together in the slow motion of a terrifying dream.

. . . Finally, a Baltimore County police officer appeared. . . . Together, she and I were able to remove the young man's shirt, exposing his chest and his terrible knife wounds. Then, the emergency medical team arrived to take the young man to a hospital. We looked into each other's eyes. . . . I saw a sense of kinship—and fear. . . . I realized that this young man and I had shared a moment that was very, very deep—and that I did not even know his name. . . .

Later, from the news reports, I learned that the name of this brave young man was Carlos Santay-Carrillo. His wife, Claudia, was in labor, preparing to give birth to their son, even as Carlos lay dying from a vicious attack. He had come to the gas station that afternoon to buy the fuel to drive his wife to the hospital.

On Mother's Day weekend, a father died in a Baltimore hospital far from his native Guatemala. A son, also named Carlos after his father, was born healthy at almost the same moment in another hospital nearby. On Mother's Day . . . , a new life, eyes not yet open, became our countryman in the promise and pain that is our America.

. . . I understand because I am a father—and because I, too, am the son of a father and mother who also traveled to Baltimore from far away in order to build a better life for their children.

To share the heart of a dying stranger is a terrible thing to bear, but it can open our own hearts to life.

I could not help but think of this man coming to the United States with hope and having it die on the concrete of a gas station. But he had brought a child into the world with a chance at a better life. *"The promise and the pain that is our America"* had taken away his dream, but given it to his son. Were we, as Americans, now going to take away another generation's hope? Were we going to not count them, or worse, cage them? Not on my watch.

CHAPTER 6

Trump's Twitter Attack on Baltimore

W e're only six months into our investigations, oversight, and reform of the administration. But we're already six months into our investigations, our oversight and reform. That's how it feels. Like we've just begun. And like we are so far behind. The urgency is constantly breathing down my neck. I feel the weight on my conscience of what must be done, of what has been allowed to continue unanswered, of what must be blunted. I feel a physical burden on my body. It is taking a toll on my health, a toll I try hard to keep from the public, the media, even from my staff and my family. Maya knows all too well. Because I can no longer climb stairs, we've had to move my bed to the living room. She gets up with me early each morning and lifts me to my feet, to get dressed, to put oversize sneakers on my gout-swollen feet, and helps me out to the car. But I cannot slow down. I cannot. We are six months in and we are already late.

For over two years I watched President Trump attack people and institutions on Twitter—Hillary Clinton, Barack Obama, John McCain, Gold Star military families, foreign leaders, NATO, the *New York Times*, the *Washington Post*, CNN, *Morning Joe*'s Joe Scarborough and Mika Brzezinski, the NFL, Chuck Schumer, Nancy Pelosi, Adam Schiff, the "Squad," judges, members of his own party, entertainers, anyone he didn't agree with. He called them names; he dismissed their credibility; he made up blatant lies; he used his thumbs as weapons of personal destruction. (We, the voters and the media, all get distracted by the nasty rhetoric and inflammatory verbiage, but what we should keep in mind is that the time and energy he spends tweeting, attacking, and bullying is time he should be spending governing, carrying out the will of the people, not on his petty personal battles.)

For whatever reason, for more than two years, he didn't go after me—even after I condemned his weak response (some called it dog-whistle approval) to the white supremacists' rally in Charlottesville, Virginia, saying there were "very fine people on both sides," even after I came down on him for pardoning Joe Arpaio, the anti-immigrant sheriff in Arizona, even after national hearings exposing his business and personal character, and the transgressions of law his administration had put in motion. Sometimes I wondered why he hadn't attacked, but mostly I wondered *when* he would. I knew it would come. It was just a matter of time, a matter of my doing enough to upset and challenge him to make me his next target. It happened loud and clear July 27, 2019. Starting at 7:14 a.m., he posted this series of tweets:

> Rep Elijah Cummings has been a brutal bully, shouting and screaming at the great men & women of Border Patrol about conditions at the Southern Border, when actually his Baltimore district is FAR WORSE and more dangerous. His district is considered the Worst in the USA. . . .

> . . . As proven last week during a Congressional tour, the Border is clean, efficient & well run, just very crowded. Cumming District is a disgusting, rat and rodent infested mess. If he spent more time in Baltimore, maybe he could help clean up this very dangerous & filthy place.

> Why is so much money sent to the Elijah Cummings district when it is considered the worst run and most dangerous anywhere in the United States. No human being would want to live there. Where is all this money going? How much is stolen? Investigate this corrupt mess immediately!

Not only was President Trump cruel, but he was, as usual, inaccurate, or just plain lying. But what is revealing is not only what he said but what had led up to it.

Trump's Twelve Steps—that led to his Twitter attack on me:

1. In January 2019, things began to heat up when the Democratic majority took the House and I took over as chair of the Oversight Committee. I officially laid out our plans to investigate the questionable security clearances of National Security Advisor Michael Flynn, aide Rob Porter, and Trump's son-in-law Jared Kushner.

2. In February, we called Michael Cohen to testify about his dealings with Trump, a blistering indictment of his former boss's business, ego, and unethical behavior.

3. In March I wrote an editorial for the *Washington Post* that called out the White House for refusing to hand us "a single piece of paper" the committee had requested, and called it "stonewalling . . . and obstruction."

4. In April the Committee subpoenaed Trump's financial records and he filed suit against not only the committee, but me personally as committee chair.

5. June was huge—we took on the battle over the citizenship question in the census and the attempt to create a fabricated rationale for it, which we exposed; then we voted to hold Attorney General William Barr and Wilbur Ross, secretary of commerce, in contempt for not providing related documents; we subpoenaed Kellyanne Conway on violations of the Hatch Act.

6. July was even bigger. We set a date for mid-month for the acting head of homeland security, Kevin McAleenan, to address the inhumane practices resulting from the "zero tolerance" immigration policy at the southern border. On July 27, we also authorized a subpoena of emails and texts

sent by Ivanka Trump, Jared Kushner, and other White House staff on their personal emails but relating to official business, arguably in violation of federal records law and White House policy.

7. Earlier in July, in preparation for the hearing, four young members, women of color—the so-called Squad—Alexandria Ocasio-Cortez, Ilhan Omar, Rashida Tlaib, and Ayanna Pressley—visited the border (so that they could come back and testify personally to the cruel treatment of immigrant families and children), at which point Trump unleashed his first anti-Squad tweet storm: "Why don't they go back and help fix the totally broken and crime infested places from which they came."

8. The Squad fired back at a press conference with Ocasio-Cortez saying, "We don't leave the things that we love . . . we propose the solutions to fix it." Nancy Pelosi and many others came to their defense.

9. On July 21, I went on *This Week* with George Stephanopoulos, and when he asked me if I thought Trump was a racist, I could not answer any other way than to say, "Yes, no doubt about it."

10. On July 24, Robert Mueller finally testified before Congress on his investigation into Russian interference in our election, contradicting the president's claim that it was a witch hunt and a hoax, refusing to exonerate the president on obstruction of justice. Nancy Pelosi, Adam Schiff, Jerry Nadler, and I addressed the media and country. It was an important day and I was passionate: "I'm begging the American people to pay attention to what is going on. . . . This is not about liking the president; it's about loving democracy. It's about loving

our country." I questioned whether the president of the United States loves our democracy. And he did not like my question one bit.

11. A few days later, a woman named Kimberly Klacik posted on Twitter a homemade video shot in West Baltimore—my district—of decaying homes and urban gloom. Fox News picked it up and invited her on *Fox & Friends*. First, they showed a clip of me grilling McAleenan about conditions at the border. Then they showed her video. Klacik, a political strategist, said, "There is a crisis at the border, but there's also a crisis in Baltimore. . . . Congressman Cummings represents the most dangerous district in America . . . abandoned row homes filled with trash, homeless addicts, empty needles . . . attracting rodents, cockroaches . . ." Not only did I find her characterization offensive, false, and inflammatory, but she didn't do her homework, or chose to ignore it, or she'd have known that the 7th District's average income and education levels are well above the national averages for majority-black areas, and the district includes such treasures as Johns Hopkins University's Hospital and Health System. Nate Silver of fivethirtyeight.com, who knows his stats better than anyone, tweeted that the district has "above average college and education rates and home prices, along with a pretty good mix of urban and suburban areas (even some rural), and well-off, working-class and middle-class areas." Yes, we have some downtrodden areas and some struggling citizens but her and Fox's portrayal was hardly an accurate, fact-based picture.

12. Within hours, Kimberly Klacik's followers went from 16,000 to 76,000. She was on national TV. Like a schoolgirl with a

crush, she said she was thrilled she got the attention of the president. President Trump viewed her posts. He saw the coverage on Fox.

And President Trump went into Twitter attack mode.

IT TOOK HIM half a year, from January to July, to go full-scale in his assault. It took minutes for the counterattack, not what the bully in the schoolyard had counted on. The immediate response didn't come from me; it came from loud, prominent voices who came to my defense and the defense of the city of Baltimore and its citizens.

As to my own retort, I purposely took some time. I gathered my thoughts and feelings. The truth is, I was hurt by what he said. Deeply hurt. This is my home. These are my friends and neighbors and voters. These are human beings, flesh and blood with feelings. With children to raise, with photos on their walls, with family dinners, with graduations to attend, with memories of the past and better hopes for the future. This man was telling them that they were less than human, that their lives were not worthwhile, their dreams would never see the light of day. He was taking away hope. That hurt them. And when they hurt, I hurt.

Then I did respond, but I would not take his bait. I would not stoop to his level. My message was my way: serious, low-key, and deeply sincere. I purposely made my statement on Twitter, to show that it could be a forum for reason, not just for hate, to show the stark comparison of our two approaches to life and our duties.

On July 27 I tweeted: "Mr. President, I go home to my district daily. Each morning, I wake up, and I go and fight for my neighbors. It is my constitutional duty to conduct oversight of the Executive Branch. But it is my moral duty to fight for my constituents. . . ." Every word was chosen carefully—not a rant, but a lesson in how to serve: "I go home to my district daily . . .— to my home, my district, my roots, never forgetting where and what I come from—daily, every single day I possibly can from DC to Baltimore, to be in my district office, to be in my home, to see my constituents' faces and hear their voices—fight for my neighbors—my neighbors, my friends, sticking up for those who cannot stick up for themselves. 'It is my constitutional duty to conduct oversight . . .'—my constitutional duty, by law, by our guiding principles. I know the constitution, Mr. President, even if you don't. It is my duty 'to conduct oversight,' to be the people's eyes and ears for what is going on, to watch over the Executive branch because no one branch is more powerful than the others. And '. . . it is my moral duty . . .' because I am guided by morality, whether you, Mr. President, are or not. I take my sacred duty very, very seriously."

Then on August 3, I spoke at the opening of a park in Baltimore, a green space, a playground—no rats, no rodents, just happy children and parents—a stark contrast to the way the president characterized my home. I told the crowd that I did not have time or patience or tolerance for people who trash my city, but I always have time for our children. "When I hear criticism by anybody about my city, I think the thing that bothers me most is that we have a situation where there are folks who are stepping on the foot, on the hope of our children. I don't know what I would have done if I'd had people in high places when I was a little boy telling me what I couldn't do. Instead, I had people telling me what I could do." Then I told the media folks who were there that I'd like President Trump to visit Baltimore, to see the real Baltimore, but of course, I doubted he would ever accept that invitation.

Meanwhile, others had already answered his attack, and they were not as restrained as I was. People on both sides of the aisle, from all parts of society and the country were outraged and vented loud and clear. I would be less than honest if I didn't say I was pleased and reassured by the outpouring of support, of fury and disgust at the president's toxic assault. No minced words. No maybes. Just honest people calling it out for what it was— racism, racism, racism—from House Speaker Nancy Pelosi— "[Cummings is] . . . a champion in the Congress and the country for civil rights and economic justice"—to candidate Elizabeth Warren to "Squad" members Rashida Tlaib—"Yo Trump, Hands off #ourchairman @RepCummings who is centered in American values that you will *never* understand"—and Ayanna Pressley to Senator Chris Van Hollen to filmmaker John Waters—"Give me the rats and roaches of Baltimore any day over the lies and racism of your Washington, Mr. Trump"—to former governor Martin O'Malley and current governor Larry Hogan to Mayor Jack Young to Jenna Bush Hager to Rev. Al Sharpton to *Morning Joe*'s Mika and Joe. Joe said, "[U]nlike the pampered son of privilege, whose rich father bought him a diag- nosis of bone spurs so he could play golf and play football and chase women while other young men of his age went to Vietnam, Elijah Cummings chose to serve through challenging times . . . he comforts people who are frightened of you."

Okay, there were some lukewarm defenses, like Mark Meadows—despite my defense of a racist labeling of him—and Rick Santorum, who both said the tweet attack was wrong, but who also let Trump off the hook as a racist.

The late-night talk show hosts weighed in. Trevor Noah, who himself is a person of color, said, "Yes, he's racist." Not "racially charged" or another euphemism. *Racist*. Seth Meyers was not subtle: "another racist outburst from a racist president." Stephen Colbert asked and answered his own question, "Previously on *Is Donald Trump Racist?* . . . Yes."

The *Baltimore Sun*'s editorial board ran a powerful retort headlined: BETTER TO HAVE A FEW RATS THAN TO BE ONE. There was no missing their message. The editorial's final paragraph could not have been better said:

Finally, while we would not sink to name-calling in the Trumpian manner . . . we would tell the most dishonest man to ever occupy the Oval Office, the mocker of war heroes, the gleeful grabber of women's private parts, the serial bankrupter of businesses, the useful idiot of Vladimir Putin and the guy who insisted there are "fine people" among murderous neo-Nazis that he's still not fooling most Americans into believing he's even slightly competent in his current post. Or that he possesses a scintilla of integrity. Better to have some vermin living in your neighborhood than to be one.

The *Sun*'s editorial was reprinted and reposted across the country. The headline even became a T-shirt.

One of the most moving defenses came from Victor Blackwell, CNN anchor, who grew up in the same district the president had targeted, my district. The morning of the Twitter blitz, Blackwell spoke right to the camera, to millions of viewers, from his heart. It was a moment of remarkable power. He quoted the president's tweet: "Cummings' district is a disgusting, rat and rodent infested mess," and then, fighting back tears, he went on:

> *"Infested."* . . . we've seen the president invoke "infestation" to criticize lawmakers before. . . . Just two weeks ago, President Trump attacked four minority Congresswomen: "Why don't they go back to the totally broken and crime *infested* places from which they came." Reminder, three of them were born here, all of them are American. *Infested, he says.* A week before his inauguration . . . [he said] "Congressman John Lewis should spend more time on fixing and helping his district, which is in horrible shape and falling apart, not to mention crime *infested*." Donald Trump has tweeted more than 43,000 times. He's insulted thousands of people. . . . But when he tweets about infestation, it's about black and brown people . . . at the height of an urgent health emergency: "Why are we sending thousands of ill-trained soldiers into Ebola *infested* areas of Africa! . . ." *Infested, he says.* "There's a revolution going on in California. So many sanctuary areas want out of this ridiculous, crime *infested* and breeding concept." *Infested, he says.* The President says about Congressman Cummings' district

that no human would want to live there. You know who did, Mr. President? I did, from the day I was brought home from the hospital to the day I left for college, and a lot of people I care about still do. There are challenges, no doubt. But people are proud of their community. . . . They care for their families there. They love their children, who pledge allegiance to the flag just like people who live in districts of congressmen who support you, sir. *They are Americans, too.*"

Victor Blackwell's tears brought me to tears. That is my city. That is Victor's city. And that is our president?

IT MEANT A lot to me to have those people come to my defense and to the defense of my city. I had been injured, wounded, knocked over—emotionally and physically. You can never picture what it is like to be assaulted, truly assaulted by the person who sits in the most powerful office in the world. You can imagine it and try to dismiss it, saying he's just a blowhard and schoolyard tough guy, using his thumbs on Twitter like fists. But the reality, the harsh cold onslaught, is just pure pain. I recall talking to someone about it at the time. I blurted out, "This hurts, it hurts, it brings me pain. So much I could be dead." This other person said, "What do you mean dead? Politically dead? No way." I said, "No! I'm talking about dead. Not alive. D-E-A-D, dead." I didn't mean some kind of expression. I meant a fact. It could kill me. I'll never know where the line is between body and soul, between head and heart, but I could feel the attack to my core. Did it make me weaker physically? No doubt. Did the support of others make me stronger in my resolve? No doubt.

I've recounted the twelve steps that preceded Trump's unleashing his hate on me and my city. But something else occurred. Something unusual to say the least. I have absolutely no proof that it was connected with Donald Trump. What I do know is that the timing was odd—coincidental, or accidental—it happened right before the president's thumbs hit the keyboard.

My house was broken into. Early the very same morning that the tweets were sent. Okay, you say, so what? You live in the inner city; it's a challenged neighborhood; crimes happen; what's out of the ordinary? Nothing.

Nothing *if* . . . If the intruder hadn't made so much noise trying to open the front door . . . and get his *bicycle* inside. That's right, he came by bicycle. And, if we presume he broke into our house to rob us, how many times do you hear a news report of a robber on a "getaway bike"? There's not much of value he could have carried away on a bike. There would be nothing out of the ordinary *if* the intruder hadn't brought his bicycle into the little vestibule entrance to my house. Why? To protect it? So it wouldn't get stolen? For a faster escape? Because he didn't want to order an Uber? It's almost funny. There would be nothing out of the ordinary *if* he had actually taken anything. Or *if* he had a weapon. (We know since our gun laws are lax, they're not hard to get.)

And *if* I, a sixty-eight-year-old man who needs a cane or a metal walker to move, hadn't been able to scare the intruder away by yelling for my wife, who ran out in time to confront the man and snap shaky iPhone photos of him hopping onto his bike and riding away. There would be nothing out of the ordinary *if* the intruder, frankly, looked more like what we think of as a robber and less like—according to my wife—a middle-aged black professional. Was I supposed to get a message from this incident? Or was he just the most incompetent robber in history? Was I supposed to be intimidated? Or was it just a coincidence that bad things happened to the bad congressman in his bad neighborhood on the day the president told everyone how bad—and infested—Cummings and Baltimore are? I don't know. I just know it happened. And nothing like that has happened in the thirty-plus years I've lived there. Not even a robber with a real weapon and a real car to drive away.

Not wanting to disturb our neighbors with sirens and flashing police lights, we waited until the morning to contact the Baltimore Police Department. I didn't say anything publicly about the break-in attempt until a few days later, on August 2. And then guess what happened? No surprise. Trump tweeted. "Really bad news! The Baltimore house of Elijah Cummings was robbed. Too bad!" Sarcastic. Mean. Typical. Which meant more backlash for his cruelty and hard heart. He earned it.

CAN YOU LOVE a place like you love a person? Or even more so? Can you love your roots, your home, and your heritage? Yes, you can. I know it because whatever Trump said about me as a person, whatever his attacks were on Elijah Cummings, none of it hurt as much as what he said about my Baltimore.

Baltimore is a place—not city limits or boundaries, but a place and space in my heart and soul—that I didn't just grow up in, but that I love. Love. Not merely like, or care for, or feel attached to, but love. It's unconditional, painful, rewarding, wrenching, uplifting, and total—like love of family. In fact, it is love of family. It is my family. I get up every morning because of this place and these people. I go to bed each night thinking of what I can do tomorrow that I didn't get done today. It isn't something to be explained; it just *is*. It is part of me like my heart and mind and my organs. For my adult life, it has been my love.

I do whatever I can do, seven days a week for anyone and everyone in the 7th District. I found scholarships for folks in the blocks of my district. I guided young men into drug rehab programs. I found health care for pregnant young women. I persuaded busy lawyers to defend people who could not afford defense. I spoke to every high school and every college I could, in order to encourage young people to strive up, to rise up, to see what is possible. Not to leave Baltimore, but to take Baltimore with them on their journey and to come back and give back. I pushed legislation for homeowners, to make home buying possible, and to prevent foreclosure, because homes keep families together, in Baltimore.

Out of that love, I set up a job fair my first week as a U.S. congressman, without outside funding, because I had promised voters I would help find them jobs. We recruited businesses to hire and applicants to show up, put them together, and hoped for a match. My very first week we did this, because that's what I promised my families. And I've sponsored an annual job fair ever since.

Later, in the aftermath of the 2008–09 housing crash, I held mortgage foreclosure prevention workshops. By 2010 and 2011, while some people in America had recovered, too many had not. Too many were in districts like mine, the last to recover from loss. There were foreclosures everywhere. And that meant boarded-up houses, decay, disease, crime—placing borderline neighborhoods at increased risk.

I knew the importance of home because I learned it at home. My parents knew that it wasn't just an address, a doorway, and some rooms. I remember when they scrimped and saved and sacrificed and prayed to buy their first home, to actually own a home. That's how important it was—not just the practical shelter and refuge but the larger meaning that it carries. Home was a place for family. Symbolic and literal. Home is almost synonymous with family. So losing your home is like losing your place in life, your family's center. It can sap the spirit out of you.

I could not accept it. So my office held workshops to teach neighbors how to hold on to their homes, how to negotiate, how to save the places for their families. When we opened the doors to those sessions, man, you could not believe the attendance. That alone told me how important this work was. It was hope in the face of loss.

What made me the angriest was the attitude that we could allow some people to be exploited. All over the country, including Baltimore and across Maryland, banks and brokers targeted people of color, and women especially, with higher-priced mortgages, that were consequently harder to keep up with, that took away what little wealth they had. They were ignored or just written off as folks who should have never been able to own a home anyway. As I said at the time, "I don't see these folks who are losing their houses as some kind of collateral damage. This is usually their biggest investment in life. . . . The people that come to me, they don't want a handout, they just want to be able to get through this storm."

I could relate, and not just from childhood. In the late 1990s, my mortgage holder started foreclosure proceedings. I was behind by six months because of other bills—child support, medical costs, taxes—the same problems everyone faces at one time or another, the problems that grow, little by little until they're huge and seem insurmountable. I managed to scrape together the money I needed. Many people aren't so fortunate.

I pushed my colleagues in Congress to look into bank and mortgage lender abuses. I pushed Fannie Mae and Freddie Mac for loan reductions for qualified borrowers. I pushed for refinancing at lower rates. I pushed for protection for service members and their families. I met with lots of resistance. Even still, my office, my staff, and I took the problems on.

And we helped people save a lot of homes. Some we could not help, and it broke my heart. To this day, every time I see a boarded-up house, I think that could have been me, or you, or my family. I cannot let it happen in my city that I love.

Sometimes it means helping many people, sometimes one at a time. Sometimes the person you help isn't indigent or a minority or what we've come to expect. It's just a person who encounters a devastating tragedy too big to endure alone. Like Katie Malone. Katie worked in my office, and one of her key jobs was helping young candidates for military academies—the Air Force, the Naval Academy, West Point—get their applications in order, with the best possible presentation of their credentials, to compete for coveted spots that could well change their lives. She put herself into her job with a fervor. When one of those young men was admitted, it was as if Katie herself got in. To say I was reliant upon her is a vast understatement.

So when I found out about the fire that took her home, I was devastated. I learned about it almost by accident, as I went into a press conference at City Hall in Baltimore. Reporters came up to me and said they were sorry about my loss. What loss? I had heard about a tragic house fire on the radio, in the car on my way, but had no idea it was my staffer, Katie Malone. I learned the details outside City Hall. The home had been completely destroyed. Six of her nine children died. I wept profusely. I could not help myself.

The fire was all over the news. And immediately there was an outpouring of support, partly because the footage of me crying was shown and reshown each time the story was told. *Congressman Cummings's staffer loses home to fire. Six children die.* People assumed Katie was black. After all, she worked for a black congressman. They assumed she was another "expected" inner-city story—single mother with nine children. But people quickly learned that she was a married, white woman, who had nine children, all by the same man, her husband, who held down a steady job. They learned that tragedy knows no color or economics or preconceptions. Loss of a home, loss of family, knows no boundaries.

I went to visit her in the hospital and when she opened her eyes and saw me, she asked me, "What's happening with Jack?" I thought to myself, Oh no, Jack must be one of her children. Then she asked me about "Devon." And "Leo." She explained that those were some of the young men she was helping with their military academy applications. Katie's life had been turned upside down; her loss was overwhelming, but she was looking out for others.

The public rallied around Katie and her husband and their kids. Donations were made. I gave her what I could. Others, many others, gave more. Her family was able to get a new home and try to start over. I do not take credit for the outpouring of support for Katie. My tears were shown and perhaps they moved people. I hope so. Money doesn't make tragedies go away. But like it or not, it is a necessity. It can help. And there is far too little of it for too many families.

Out of love for my city and my people, I have given away money I didn't have more times than I can count—and more money than I can count. It's well worth it. One day, a few years into my congressional service, I met a woman at a local wedding, an elderly, frail woman who was lugging around an oxygen tank bigger than she was. Her face had such a worried look that I asked her what was wrong. She said she'd been gone from home that day much longer than she expected and was running low on oxygen. She told me about her medical condition and how she couldn't live without oxygen, but she couldn't carry any more with her because this tank was already too much to handle. I asked her if she knew about something called Inogen, which I'd just heard about from my wife, who had discovered it during a Google search. It's a small, portable oxygen device you can plug in and recharge wherever you are. She said, yes, she'd heard of it, and it sounded like a miracle.

I said to her, "Well, why don't you get one and then you wouldn't be dragging this elephant around behind you?"

She asked me how much it cost. When I told her three thousand dollars, she just shook her head sadly.

I know, that's a lot for air. But I couldn't leave her that way. One of my office staff was sitting next to me at the wedding and I asked him for a pen. He knew what was going to happen next and he tried to catch my eye to maybe get me to reconsider, but he also knew there was no stopping me. I reached for my wallet and took out a blank check I carry, asked the woman her name, started to write, and then stopped and said, "If I give you two thousand dollars, can you come up with the rest?"

She nodded, with tears running down her cheeks. I told her my staffer would help her order the device. She called me about two weeks later and I'll never forget her words: "I'm free." What went through my mind was the phrase from the Declaration of Independence, "the pursuit of happiness." I think people are entitled to the pursuit of happiness. That's freedom.

Out of that love for my city, more than twenty years ago I began the Elijah Cummings Youth Leadership Program, to spread the love to another generation, across barriers, across ethnic boundaries. In twenty years, we've sent more than two hundred young African-Americans from Baltimore to Israel, all from the congressional district.

These young people, tenth graders, first go through a rigorous selection process, then a yearlong leadership development phase. They're mentored by leaders here and in Washington, D.C. Then they spend a full month in Israel, touring Jerusalem, Tel Aviv, Nazareth, and the Dead Sea, sharing the experience of living in another culture, a culture that survived the Holocaust, a culture that is under threat daily in the Middle East, a culture that has nurtured its past and protected its future. The parallels to these kids and their heritage are clear. In the third year, these young people put their experience to work back home, in the community service phase, mentoring other kids, middle school children in our district, sharing and spreading the culture, showing another generation how to reach out beyond themselves, past barriers, to see what is possible.

They go for free. Otherwise it would never happen. The program was built on a contribution from Jerry Hoffberger, former owner of the Baltimore Orioles and a prominent Jewish philanthropist. And it was built on my own belief that I echoed this past year on our twentieth anniversary: "I want to send a message that we cannot as African-Americans progress without coalitions, and our greatest coalition partner has been the Jewish people in America."

Does it succeed? No question. It has touched hundreds of lives, those who went, those they mentored, their families and neighbors. The same Victor Blackwell, the CNN weekend news anchor who spoke so passionately about his city and me when Trump attacked Baltimore—he was one of the first selected for the program more than twenty years ago.

MY LOVE OF my home, of my family, empowers me. I do my best to protect it against threat, abuse, or ambush by anyone. Attack my city, you attack me. Early in the summer, long before the president's assault, I was invited to speak at the National Press Club and we set a date for early August. That's usually a slow time in Washington, D.C., not when you can expect to draw a big turnout, especially among the media. Like the rest of us, they go on vacation in the summer. But that was before the president's rat-infested rant. That was before the backlash. By early August, by the time of the speech, it was the fuel and fire that would power my words and would guarantee attendance and attention. That and two more horrible, tragic events—the mass shootings in El Paso, Texas, and Dayton, Ohio—communities half a country away from Baltimore, yet faced with the same vulnerabilities.

A little before 11 a.m., on August 3, 2019, a gunman, armed with a semiautomatic AK-47, began firing off shots in an El Paso Walmart parking lot. Shooting nonstop, he then entered the store in El Paso, and eventually killed 22 people and injured 24 more, the deadliest shooting of the year. The store manager saw the parking lot shootings and called a "Code Brown," an active shooter alert. Active shooter alerts, school drills to run for cover, and first responders rushing to shooting scenes are routines that we didn't even have in America a few years ago, things that we've all come to accept like traffic signals at intersections, as if they are normal. But they aren't. Or they shouldn't be. There's nothing normal about this. To make matters even uglier, this mass shooting was later suspected to be a hate crime, white nationalist violence aimed at Hispanic-Americans. The shooter bought the gun from Romania, the ammunition from Russia, and by today's laws, it was all legal. Why? Why would it be legal for someone, anyone, to just order a gun from Romania and bullets from Russia?

That same day, only a few hours after El Paso, a man in suburban Dayton, Ohio, in a nightclub area, wearing a mask and body armor, fired his weapon into a crowd, killing nine people and injuring more than twenty others. He himself was killed by police within seconds of his attack. Acquaintances described him as "an outcast" who had been arrested and had made threats. Investigators found evidence of his writings that exposed an interest in mass killing. Both shooters had histories that would call into question their access to firearms. Both had no trouble getting weapons. Why is that okay in America? How long would we wring our hands and do nothing? How many times could we say the victims have our hopes and prayers? When would we do something besides hope and pray? How long would we fail the people?

Those tragedies, those injustices, were in my thoughts when I spoke in Washington four days later. Thanks to Donald Trump and his declaration of war on me and my home, thanks to our national outrage and sorrow over gun violence, thanks to my committee's relentless investigations, a late summer speech that normally would have drawn a modest showing and modest media coverage barely enough to fill a small room at the National Press Club became the hottest ticket in town. It had to be moved to the largest room at the Press Club. The place was packed: cameras, microphones, reporters, national anchors, and investigative reporters. I had a lot to say. And I was determined to say it.

But I almost didn't get my chance. I had been feeling bad, very bad, tired and worn down. Against my doctor's urging, and my wife's, I hadn't let up. We had a job to do. Hearings to hold. Truth to find. I worked early; I worked late; I drafted and reviewed legislation; I returned emails in the middle of the night; I conferred with colleagues at all hours. Finally, after weeks of pushing too hard, in late July, I nearly collapsed.

My wife took my temperature; it was 102 and she called the

doctor. He sent me right to the hospital, where I was told I had pneumonia. He said, "Elijah, you better take care of yourself now if you have any hope of doing your job in the future."

I was still in a hospital bed at Johns Hopkins the morning of my speech, on IV fluids and meds, barely able to move. My wife asked me what I was going to do, but I think she knew.

"I'm going to give that speech if I have to crawl," I said.

I did not crawl, but I didn't run, either. I managed to convince the medical team to give me a "four-hour pass," which is just what it sounds like: highly restricted, controlled conditions, with time limitations that I could not break. I was allowed to go to Washington with medical care nearby, then give my speech, do a Q-and-A, and get back to the hospital in four hours, not a minute longer. My car arrived at the Press Club; I was wheeled into the room, assisted to my seat on the dais. When my time to speak came, I had to be helped to my feet and a stool was placed near the podium just in case I had to sit. After that, I didn't need any more help. I had already gone through the ritual I follow before every speech. I rehearse with God. I look out at the audience, I soak them in, I get a "feel" for the place and time, the moment. I was ready. That speech, that day, was my destiny. I had always treated every speech as if it was my last. Today that was more true than any before.

I stood quietly and looked out at the faces. I waited. I breathed. And then I spoke: "God has called me to this moment. I did not ask for it." I had been brought there by my pain—in body and spirit—which had fueled my passion—my mission—and no question about it, I had a purpose. Yes, I had a true purpose that day. I had summoned my strength for a reason. I was there to deliver a message to the messengers—the media—to carry back to their readers and listeners and followers and bloggers and posters. I wanted them to hear the hue and cry of our people against the injustices, the cruelty, the divisiveness that were all fast becoming commonplace, almost normal. I wanted the messengers to hear the message and shout it out to everyone and say, "No! We will not let it happen! No! We're better than this. We're so much better than this." I recounted the horrors of the gun violence of El Paso and Dayton and our failure as a government to do anything about it, anything but offer prayers and inadequate sorrow. I decried our letting people die because they couldn't afford the medicines that could keep them alive, and our failure to do anything about it. I retold the story of my ten-year-old niece, hearing of the cruelty to immigrant children and the border, asking me, "Uncle Elijah, are they going to put us in cages?" and our failure to do anything to stop that brutality. I relived the attacks the president had levied against me and my city and so many others, attacks we all know are ugly, and evil and immoral . . . and our failure to do anything about them. I railed, loud and full-throated against the stonewalling on documents and testimony, flaunting subpoenas, ignoring the Constitution, assailing our right to vote, threatening our democracy, and our failure to do anything about it.

But we—the people and the free press—can do something about it. We are not powerless. I reminded the messengers of their duty to report and inform, over and over, relentlessly. Right now more than ever. I invoked Martin Luther King's words, "our silence becomes our betrayal." I told them not to be silent. I told them to speak up. I said, I know they were told to turn off their cell phones when they came in but I said no, they should turn them on, then and there. They should text and email and tweet to get the messages out—to legislators, to readers, to preachers, to everyone they could. I said loud and clear, "This is a fight for the soul of our democracy." It hit home. I knew it by the repeated interruptions of applause and shout-outs. They applauded, and they stood, and they applauded more. I told them how much I appreciated their support. I was humbled. And tired. So tired. But I wasn't quite done.

We had the Q-and-A until I had answered every question I possibly could. I had stayed to the limit of my pass, perhaps longer. It was time to keep my promise and make my way to Johns Hopkins. When I got back to the hospital, I was spent. I crawled back into my bed and lay there for hours and days, recovering from that short journey. But it was worth it. It was worth the pain to refuel the passion in order to pursue the purpose. I was rewarded with accolades over the next few days. To each one, I responded the same: "Thank you for your words. But more than your words, I need your help."

Baltimore and Maryland got a dose of help from very close to home. Without telling me about it, my wife, my soul mate, Dr. Maya Rockeymoore Cummings, chair of the Maryland Democratic Party, wrote an op-ed two days later. She went beyond my speech. She tied Trump's ugly words to the gun violence it spurs, and then connected the dots to the damage he was wreaking in Maryland and across the country, and turned that into an exhortation to vote! Maya called the president out for his "verbal cluster bombs" and put into words that we have all thought to ourselves: "Donald J. Trump's offensive language may have influenced the gunmen." She labeled his "toxic brand of racism, sexism, classism, and xenophobia . . . [as] driving a disturbing increase in hate crimes." She minced no words on his "erratic leadership style . . . his overestimation of his negotiating skills . . . an ill-advised trade war . . ." And she urged us to action: "coming together to vote him out of office would also be a major win-win for Maryland's people."

Maya, well said. So well said. I read it from my hospital bed and it went a long way toward my healing. Each day I thought I'd be stronger and go home or go back to the Hill "tomorrow." Tomorrow stretched into the day after. And the day after. I never stopped working. I worked from my hospital bed. I had meetings in my room. I made conference calls and signed subpoenas. I attended the Democratic caucus sessions by phone. Then, blessedly, Congress went on recess.

I am not feeling sorry for myself. I rarely do. (As they say, what's the point?) I have what I want in life. My work. My voters. My home. My family. I don't want money. I never have, which is fine, because I have rarely had much. I own a few suits, ties, and dress shirts, and a pair of good shoes—the uniform of my job—and sneakers and sweats for weekends. I have a large television, a simple, comfortable car for driving back and forth from D.C. to Baltimore, and of course, a cell phone, which I seem to wear out each year. Since I shaved my head a few years ago, I don't even spend money on haircuts. My needs are modest. That's good because my government salary gets stretched thin—a little to a neighbor's kid's school fundraiser, or a gift for one of my daughters, or a contribution to my church, and, not as often as I should, some flowers for my wife. But I have no complaints. Plenty of people around me are struggling. I can't live high on the hog when I know they can't. They're my family. My reward is in my work. For better or worse, there's always more to do. That keeps me going. That and Maya.

CHAPTER 7

Impeachment— Not If, but When

July and August are hot and muggy and thick in Washington. The air is actually heavy. You can feel it. In late summer and into fall of 2019, the air was heavy with change. You could feel it, too. I sensed the next few months were going to be different in Congress and for the country, and for me personally, maybe the most critical time I'd faced in my life. A word that had been whispered and threatened almost since Donald Trump came down the escalator at Trump Tower to announce his run for president became real: impeachment.

For two full years, he'd governed, if we can call it that, with a total disregard for or ignorance of the system, of the Constitution, and of democracy. Like a petulant child, he called people names, people on all sides—Crooked Hillary, Lyin' Ted Cruz, Crazy Bernie Sanders, Little Marco Rubio, Pocahontas/Elizabeth Warren, Low IQ Maxine Waters, Slippery James Comey, the Squad, Mr. Magoo/Jeff Sessions, Conflicted Bob Mueller, Rocket Man Kim Jong-Un, and of course, Fake News. And he didn't leave me out, King Elijah. Trump had the highest turnover of members of his administration in history—fired, pushed out, or fed up with working for him, too many to list but to name just a few: Chiefs of Staff Reince Priebus and John Kelly; strategist Steve Bannon; National Security Advisors Michael Flynn, H. R. McMaster, and John Bolton; Press Secretaries Sean Spicer and Sarah Sanders; Directors of Communication Anthony Scaramucci and Hope Hicks; National Security Council member Fiona Hill; National Economic Council member Gary Cohn; Office of Public Liaison member Omarosa Manigault; White House Counsels Don McGahn and Ty Cobb; personal attorney John Dowd; chair of the Opioid Commission Chris Christie; cabinet secretaries and independent agencies— Mike Young (Agriculture); James Mattis and Patrick Shanahan (Defense); Tom Price (Health and Human Services); John Kelly, Elaine Duke, Kirstjen Nielsen, and Kevin McAleenan (Homeland Security); Ryan Zinke (Interior); Jeff Sessions, Sally Yates, Matthew Whitaker, and Rod Rosenstein (Justice or attorneys general); James Comey and Andrew McCabe (FBI); Alexander Acosta and Patrick Pizzella (Labor); Rex Tillerson (State); Nikki Haley (UN); David Shulkin, Robert Wilkie, and Peter O'Rourke (Veterans Affairs); Scott Pruitt (EPA), Walter Shaub

(Ethics); and literally hundreds more. Trump abandoned long-time allies—NATO, Mexico, Australia, even Canada; cozied up to tyrants—Kim Jong-Un, Erdogan of Turkey, and, most flagrantly, Vladimir Putin; threatened to unseat or "primary" Republicans who questioned him; gave a "dog-whistle" approval to white supremacists after the Unite the Right rally in Charlottesville; and encouraged/pushed world leaders to stay at Trump properties around the world. We had never seen a leader act like this in our lifetimes, at least not in a democracy.

Private whispers and some wishful thinking on the impeachment of Trump go back to even before he took office. What had been a rumble was now a roar.

During his first two years as president, the appetite for impeachment grew day by day, from hushed what-ifs to open threats. Only one month into the new presidency, with Republican majorities controlling both Houses in the 115th Congress, a PAC to impeach Trump was formed. By May 2017, the firing of FBI director James Comey—when he wouldn't drop the investigation of Michael Flynn—led to talk in Congress of an "impeachment clock," or countdown. Richard Blumenthal of Connecticut, Maxine Waters of California, and Angus King of Maine each separately hinted at impeachment. Even Republican John McCain of Arizona said events were getting to "Watergate scope and size." In May 2017, one of the earliest voices for impeachment was Al Green of Texas. In private, among the Democratic leadership, there was plenty of agreement with the movement, but publicly and strategically, most of us agreed we should proceed carefully and cautiously.

Events reinforced the strategy of letting the evidence build over time. In May, Robert Mueller, former director of the FBI, was made special counsel to investigate Russian interference in the 2016 election and possible cooperation or collusion by the Trump campaign, appointed by Deputy Attorney General Rod Rosenstein (after Attorney General Jeff Sessions recused himself, infuriating his boss, the president). In June, a copy of Comey's congressional testimony came out showing that the president pushed Comey to "let go" of his investigation of Flynn, and pressured Comey for his personal loyalty. Comey replied only that he would give "honest loyalty" to the president. Shortly after, Comey was fired.

That was enough to cause Brad Sherman of California to join Al Green in drafting articles of impeachment, introduced to the House in July 12, 2017, accusing President Trump of obstruction of justice in the investigation of Russian election interference. In August, after the rally in Charlottesville, Steve Cohen of Tennessee added articles of impeachment, stating that Trump had "failed the presidential test of moral leadership."

At the same time an independent impeachment movement was led by billionaire Tom Steyer that gained more than one million signatures just in the month of October, then almost two million by November and over six million a year later. Al Green introduced on December 6, 2017, a resolution to impeach the president. He introduced another resolution to impeach on January 19, 2018.

Up to this point, as the minority party in Congress, most of the Democratic leadership, myself included, were against formal action on impeachment. Our strategy was to keep pursuing and gathering damning and irrefutable evidence before taking the fateful step of impeachment. In 2017, when Nancy Pelosi was still minority leader, she spoke to the Democratic caucus regularly to discuss and strategize. She put in countless phone calls at all hours to the key ranking members who, if we won the House, would become the pivotal committee chairs on impeachment—Adam Schiff (Intelligence), Jerry Nadler (Judicial), Maxine Waters (Finance), and me (Oversight). She asked questions, floated strategy, thought ahead, always ahead.

Elijah, it's Nancy. Sorry to call so late/early . . .
It's Nancy, tell me what your sense of timing is . . .
Here's what we learned from Mueller . . .
Will Flynn tell us anything? . . .
Will Hope Hicks? . . .
Any Republicans coming our way . . .
We don't *want* to impeach; it's a last resort . . .
No inflammatory rhetoric . . .

Nancy Pelosi uses power—in this case minority power—with what can only be called wisdom. She listens, she processes, she acts . . . wisely. She always pays close attention to the public, our constituents, the people we work for. The public was moving toward the possibility of impeachment but moving slowly and steadily—30 percent in favor in February 2018, almost 40 percent by midsummer, mostly among Democrats, of course, but along with Trump's popularity in his own party dropping significantly. As leaders, we kept the math of what impeachment and conviction would require front and center in our plans. A majority of the House can pass articles of impeachment but it takes two-thirds of the Senate to convict. We thought we might take the House back at the midterms but were realistic in assuming the Senate would still be controlled by the Republicans.

In the November midterm elections we did take the House in a blue wave. With it came a growing fervor among our members to be more aggressive on impeachment. With the majority in the House, when the new term began, we would have real clout. But to me and others at the forefront, that was all the more reason to use it wisely. On December 6, 2017, again Al Green proposed articles of impeachment, this time accusing Trump of "Associating the Presidency with White Nationalism, Neo-Nazism and Hatred" and "Inciting Hatred and Hostility." We, as Democratic leaders, were not ready to embrace the move, stating, "legitimate questions have been raised about Trump's fitness to lead this nation" but it is "not the time to consider articles of impeachment" in light of investigations by Congress and the special counsel. Coupled with the fact that the Republicans were still in control of the House until the new Congress was sworn in in January, the resolution was defeated.

During the midterm campaigns, naturally impeachment had been a big issue, on both sides. In liberal and swing districts where it appealed to Democrats and independents, the Democratic candidates invoked it often. In more conservative districts, Republican candidates used it as a rallying cry to defend the president. In "purple areas," those that had been Democratic in the past but had gone for Trump in 2016, it was more delicate for both sides. On balance, it probably helped the Democrats, because Trump's day-to-day conduct, constantly nasty, constantly threatening, constantly shameful, fueled doubt, disappointment, and sometimes outright regret.

We thought he was going to drain the swamp. But now the swamp is deeper and dirtier than ever.

IN JANUARY 2019, when the Democrats became the majority in the House, Nancy Pelosi became the Speaker; Schiff was made chair of Intelligence; Nadler took over Judiciary; and I had Oversight. Typical of Pelosi, these choices were not rewards for service or her personal favorites; they were prudent, tactical picks, each made with future strategy in mind. Jerry Nadler is a tough, self-made guy, a scholar—with a Yeshiva education—a smart lawyer who worked his way through law school at night, who climbed every rung of the political ladder, no silver-spoon life, for sure. Adam Schiff is just plain brilliant, a valedictorian in high school—most likely to succeed—who went to Stanford and then Harvard Law, and became an assistant U.S. attorney (prosecuting a famous case against an FBI agent for spying for the Soviets). Nancy Pelosi was well aware of Schiff's courtroom skills—understated, totally prepared, never surprised, relentless—and was thinking ahead to where the impeachment process might take us, and who might take the lead in it. She had spoken to me on more than one occasion about whether I could take a prominent role—could I be *the* lead—and she and I both knew that given my unpredictable health, the answer was likely no. Schiff was the designated commander even before impeachment was official. They don't come better than Adam.

We went to work. We had a lot to do. We were determined to do it right. The first decision was a restatement of our previous stance on impeachment to wait—wait for the report of the special counsel. In March, when asked about our position by the *Washington Post*, Pelosi delivered a brilliant summary: "I'm not for impeachment; impeachment is so divisive to the country that unless there's something so compelling and overwhelming and bipartisan [what might come out of the Mueller Report], I don't think we should go down that path, because it divides the country. And he's just not worth it. No. I don't think he is. I mean, ethically unfit, intellectually unfit, curiosity-wise unfit. No, I don't think he's fit to be president of the United States."

Trump tweeted back his thanks for her statement: "I greatly appreciate Nancy Pelosi's statement against impeachment, but everyone must remember the minor fact that I never did anything wrong . . . and impeachment is for 'high crimes and misdemeanors.'" Evidently he didn't read, or comprehend, Nancy's whole statement. He must have missed "ethically unfit, intellectually unfit, curiosity-wise unfit. . . . I don't think he's fit to be president of the United States." People around the president readily admit he rarely reads anything and doesn't absorb much of what he does read.

We simply went on with our plan to investigate, investigate, investigate. In January, Trump's former personal lawyer and convicted felon Michael Cohen agreed to address my committee.

Later in January, the inspector general of the General Services Administration, the department that keeps track of costs and practices regarding business dealings within the federal government, reported that the president may be in violation of the emoluments clause of the Constitution. The way I see it, what the emoluments clause means, in plain English, is that no one holding federal office can receive a gift, payment, or anything of value from a foreign state or ruler or representative. For example, the president of the United States can't or shouldn't accept money or payment, directly or through a company he owns, from a government official—president, prime minister, king, queen, emissary, dignitary, ambassador, etc.—who is visiting and staying at, eating at, or playing golf at one of the president's hotels, resorts, condos, or whatever. As of June 2019, NBC said at least twenty-two foreign governments had spent money at Trump Organization properties (not to mention more than two hundred other government-involved companies, lobbyists, political organizations, and other influential groups). That's what the emoluments clause is all about. The way I see it, those are all violations. Plain and simple.

In February, as promised, Michael Cohen did address the Committee on Oversight and Reform for seven hours.

In mid-March, the Mueller Report was turned over to Attorney General William Barr who jumped the gun by interpreting the investigation's conclusions and determining that it did not contain evidence sufficient to support obstruction of justice. In fact, that was Barr's personal opinion and not the word or words of the report. But given his position as the highest legal officer in the United States, a lot of people took it to be true. That, in itself, may turn out to be a violation of duty or law. A few days later, Rashida Tlaib introduced another resolution for a formal impeachment investigation. The Mueller Report was made public, and in it the investigators list multiple incidents involving Trump that could constitute obstruction of justice. Mueller opted not to accuse the president, nor did he or his report exonerate the president from obstruction, instead letting Congress make that determination. That decision by Mueller has been examined, questioned, second-guessed, and just plain not understood. But it was Mueller's call.

Meantime, outside investigation and enforcement bodies like the Southern District of New York could also pursue the possible crimes on their own.

In October 2019 Republican Justin Amash of Michigan (who later changed his party affiliation to independent) came down hard on what he felt was Barr's misinterpretation of the findings, and was the first GOP member to call for impeachment based on obstruction.

Once the Democrats were in the majority of the 116th Congress, the resolutions to impeach built steam. On March 1, 2019, Brad Sherman and Al Green introduced another resolution. On March 27, Rashida Tlaib, joined by Green, did so again. In the summer, Sheila Jackson Lee of Texas joined with Al Green in introducing yet another such resolution. Each time there was a roll call vote; each time the resolutions were defeated.

Personally, throughout the process, I met and talked with my most aggressive colleagues, often the youngest, newest members, the next generation of Democrats. I understood their outrage and their drive. I shared it. Over and over, I counseled them, do not stifle your intentions or your purpose, but use your energy to keep at the task, adding evidence on evidence, witness on witness, act on act. We must do everything we can to put together an ironclad case, a case even a Republican majority in the

Senate will have to take seriously. Make a case of behavior that the American people find un-American.

Day after day, you could feel the fever in the House rising. The representatives—Democrats and some Republicans—could feel that fever among their constituents. The media reported on the rising temperature daily, even hourly. Then the thermometer almost burst.

I know heat—the literal heat of temperature and human heat of mistreatment. I knew it, and felt it, from the time I was a little kid. Baltimore is hot in the summer, as hot as you can imagine, especially without air-conditioning, or on a front stoop, or out on the streets. And living on the edge of poverty, that's a kind of heat, too. Stifling heat. That was how I grew up. But I learned something simple about it. Do something. What do you mean, do something? I mean make an effort. Do something small. My father, every single Friday, on payday, stopped on his way home and bought my mother a flower and a Baby Ruth candy bar. He couldn't buy her a dozen roses or a big bouquet so he bought one flower. And one candy bar, one Baby Ruth, because her name was Ruth. That's all he could do but for years later, after he died, if you mentioned the flower and the candy bar to my mother, she wept. It was everything to her. When it seems like you can't do anything, do something. Don't say it's too big or too oppressive to overcome. Start. Try. Now. As my grandmother said to me, "Elijah, don't let them make us wait anymore." That's the message we were getting from the people of the country, "don't wait anymore." Do something. You may not get all the way, but you may get somewhere.

THERE IS AN old adage that says, "The wheels of justice turn slowly but grind exceedingly fine." I might add "especially in a democracy." And we could add still further, "especially in a government built on checks and balances, on the separation of powers." When one arm of government, say the executive, is fundamentally at odds with another arm, the legislature, often the only resolution comes from the third arm, the judiciary. It's basic civics, something that almost everyone in public service understands. *Almost* everyone. The forty-fifth president of the United States does not understand civics, and when he is forced to deal with it, he doesn't like it. Those wheels just keep turning, slowly, yes, but relentlessly on and on and on. Sometimes the wheels speed up. Sometimes a great deal of justice is achieved almost all at once. The period of August 26 through October 7, 2019, was one of those times.

In less than six weeks, in the world of Washington, D.C., the world of Donald Trump, and the world of American democracy, the following happened:

First, a whistle-blower filed a complaint alleging that the president and his attorney Rudy Giuliani attempted to trade aid to a foreign government in exchange for that government (Ukraine) agreeing to dig up dirt to discredit a family member of one of the president's likely opponents in the upcoming election, that is, finding damning information on Hunter Biden, son of Democratic candidate Joe Biden.

Then . . . the "rough" transcript of the telephone conversation between Trump and the head of that country (Volodymyr Zelensky, president of Ukraine) verifying an apparent request for a "favor" to trade aid for dirt was turned over to Congress—a quid pro quo.

Then . . . a second whistle-blower came forward, seeking protection under the law, claiming to have further firsthand knowledge of the same phone conversation.

Then . . . testimony before congressional committees was set for multiple State Department officials familiar with the Ukraine-U.S. dealings, including current and recently dismissed diplomatic personnel (by the president).

Then . . . two associates of Rudy Giuliani, the president's personal attorney, were arrested for campaign finance violations in connection with an effort to recall the United States ambassador to Ukraine. A separate investigation of Giuliani for alleged campaign finance violations was commenced. (Keep in mind, Giuliani is Trump's personal attorney, not authorized to conduct foreign policy or an overlap of foreign policy and business.)

Then . . . three court decisions went against the president: The president's lawyers were turned down in their attempts to prevent his financial records from being produced (one based on the request from my committee, the other from the federal Southern District of New York). Another decision blocked Trump's immigration moves to withhold green cards from anyone who utilized public benefits (judges in four states agreed this was simply discrimination against poor people). And the courts rejected Trump's scheme to use $3.6 billion in Pentagon funds designated for military purposes to build his border wall.

Then . . . Kevin McAleenan, the fourth head of homeland security in the Trump presidency, and whom my committee had interviewed on the barbaric treatment of immigrant families at the border, submitted his resignation, condemning the "tone, the message, the public face and approach" of the administration's immigration policy, that is, Trump's personal language.

Then . . . Trump's own party leaders broke with him on his decision to pull U.S. military support out of Syria, opening the Syrian Kurds to attack by Turkish forces, and virtually inviting ISIS to rebuild. Even Trump's most loyal yes-men and -women rebelled against the move—Lindsey Graham, Mitch McConnell, Nikki Haley, and some of Trump's red-meat talk radio loyalists.

Then . . . to top it all off, Fox News, Donald Trump's personal favorite media channel, issued a poll showing that 51 percent of the population favored impeachment and removal from office.

Yes, it was a very bad few weeks. Those wheels of justice ground slowly, but oh so fine. The demand for impeachment was growing and growing.

Was it over? No. But it lived up to the words of Robert Kennedy, "Democracy is messy. And it's hard." Welcome to reality, Mr. Trump. This is civics. This is justice. This is democracy.

Shortly thereafter, the House began to call witnesses and begin the informal process of inquiry. Over the next several days, Gordon Sondland, the ambassador to the European Union, was blocked from testifying by the White House; the White House said deadlines for turning over documents were unreasonable; Giuliani associates and Russian operatives Lev Parnas and Igor Fruman were named to be deposed; the former ambassador to Ukraine did testify; the deadline for Sondland documents came and went unmet; Vice President Pence and the State Department and the Office of Management and Budget all refused to meet document deadlines; a former advisor to Secretary of State Mike Pompeo testified; and finally the ambassador to the European Union was deposed and testified.

In the midst of it all, on October 15, the second Democratic presidential debate was held but the inquiry process did not slow down. We and the nation watched as the candidates fielded questions on impeachment, whistle-blowers, Ukraine, and quid pro quo—especially Joe Biden—and we got right back to our investigative work.

I WAS NOT present for any of these moments. I was back in the hospital and I had never been sicker in my life. My cancer had come back. As always, my staff and I managed to keep it quiet and private, without media attention, without even a leak. That was important, because as I told Maya many times when I had a setback, we had to keep it quiet, unknown to the vultures—the political opposition or even those on the same side who wanted my seat—who were always circling, looking for weakness. It's the nature of politics, an ugly blood sport, literally. My condition had become a reality, like an unwanted visitor, something I would just live with, and my loved ones—my daughters, my staff, and my Maya—would live through it with me, and the key word is "live" because that was me, that was in my soul—live day-to-day, do as much as you can, keep fighting, don't worry about what if, just keep going.

No, my cancer was never gone, but in the past it would let me win a few battles, fool me into thinking I could outlast it. Now it would not be denied. It was back with a vengeance.

That is what it took to keep me away. Still, I sent and received emails to and from my office on the Hill. Still, I signed
letters and subpoenas. During this time, I spoke daily with
Nancy Pelosi on the grounds on which to base the articles of
impeachment. I talked to Jerry Nadler and Adam Schiff on
strategy and tactics. We worked daily on the preparation of our
case, on evidence we would need, on documents to request,
on witness lists. Each of our committees had responsibilities,
details, records. And I was not about to abdicate mine at such
a crucial time. I worked early and late. I worked from my bed.
In fact, plenty of people swore they saw me on the Hill or in my
office or on a television interview—that's how hard and long I
was working.

My doctors were not happy.

My wife was not happy.

My daughters were not happy.

But they all knew me by now. They knew this was Elijah
Cummings and, sick or not, I would not shirk my duty. But I
paid for it dearly. Drained of energy, unable to stand up, barely
able to lift a spoon, sometimes gasping just to form a sentence.

I called my chief of staff, Vernon Simms, and told him to
bring me the envelope, the one I had given him two years ago,
when I'd gone in for heart surgery, the one he had tried to give
back to me so many times, the one for Maya. On our phone call,
I told him, "Vernon, I am tired. So tired. I have to leave. I just
have to leave."

He asked to speak to Maya. I knew he was asking her if I was
saying I had to leave the hospital or leave, leave this earth. I

heard her tell Vernon the truth, that I was saying I was ready to leave this earthly world.

As I spoke to God each morning and night, I knew I was losing this battle. I prayed we would not lose the battle for our democracy.

CHAPTER 8

The Last Chapter

On October 17, 2019, at 2:30 a.m., Elijah Cummings, sixty-eight, died. His doctors had told him less than forty-eight hours earlier that his cancer had spread throughout his body. There was no more they or anyone could do. Elijah Cummings was moved to hospice for his final hours. During that time, he was visited by his family. His wife, Maya, was by his bed. She reflected on their life and those last hours.

When Elijah and I first met on Capitol Hill in 1997, it was hardly romantic. It was all business back then. I was a Congressional Black Caucus fellow assigned to the office of former congressman Mel Watt. Beginning in 1998 I started collecting data for my dissertation: the African-American political response to HIV/AIDS—a study of the Congressional Black Caucus and the 105th Congress. Congressman Watt's chief of staff, Joyce Brayboy, offered to help me secure interviews. Congressman Cummings was one of the first to reply to the request for interviews about the dissertation. I went to his office and we talked about the issue. He was very familiar with the challenge of HIV/AIDS, having already worked diligently on finding solutions. I asked him why he cared so much and he talked about black men from his church, literally just disappearing, how he felt like he had to do something because people were dying.

I asked him about the stigma—the gay disease. He said, "Stigma? That doesn't matter to me at all. It's about making sure that people can hold on to life."

In my mind, I immediately labeled him a transformational leader, someone who was at the forefront at that time of a very tough issue, whose mind wasn't tainted by the stigma or stereotypes.

After that, I didn't see much of the congressman. I ended up staying on the Hill working, first for the House Ways and Means Committee, the Social Security subcommittee, and then I became New York congressman Charlie Rangel's assistant/chief of staff/senior policy advisor.

Early on, when I would see Elijah around the Capitol we

would say hello, nothing more. I was with Rangel a year and a half. But after a while, when we saw each other, Elijah became very friendly and our conversations were easy, almost like we had known each other for a million years. He got into the habit of coming to sit next to me in meetings, outside of meetings, at receptions, in the House cafeteria, with the ease of old friends. But nothing romantic, even remotely.

Then one sunny day my sister came to the Hill to visit me and I took her on a tour of D.C. Afterward, we were sitting outside under a tree between the Capitol and the House office buildings when who should come ambling by but Elijah. I introduced him to my sister, and told him that she was a newly minted medical student at Johns Hopkins. They started talking about Hopkins since it was in the congressman's district and he knew all the big players there.

Then out of the blue, and uncharacteristically for him, he said to my sister, "Your sister [gesturing toward me] won't go out with me."

Equally uncharacteristically for me, I said, "Well, you've never asked."

He had never even hinted. I guess this was his way of asking. He was sort of using the audience with my sister as his cover. It made me laugh at his almost boyishness. He didn't ask right then, in front of my sister, but he did not long after.

We scheduled to go out—and I mean scheduled because his life was so packed with obligations and meetings and speeches and mine was pretty busy, too. We went on a real date, a first date, back in 2000. But it really became the beginning of a long and strong friendship. It was a friendship for good reasons—we connected personally but I found out he was already in a relatively committed relationship . . . or maybe two. So, we ended up becoming fast friends, over several years. I was not in a committed relationship myself, just dating other people on and off. But he and I would talk; he'd call or I'd call and we would talk for hours. There were times that we would back off and not talk for months. Then we'd reconnect, like an old friend. That just kept going, on and off, more on than off. That was around 2005, five years after he had finally asked me out, a very long courtship or friendship-courtship. Little by little, phone call by phone call, occasional date by occasional date, and then with more and more time spent together, it slowly, steadily blossomed into a real love affair. And our romance turned into a marriage on June 20, 2008.

I remember his way of asking me to marry him. It was very Elijah-like. We had been engaged for a while, with no wedding date or details. I was supposed to give a talk at the Rollins School of Public Health at Emory University in Atlanta on that Friday morning. He drove me to the airport and casually said, "When you get back from Atlanta, do you want to get married this afternoon?"

I just laughed and said, "Sure."

I think he'd already gotten the paperwork a while before. Somewhere along the trip, between flying down and speaking and flying back, I called my girlfriend Callie Jackson Rahman from college and her husband, Gary, and asked them if they would show up at the house that night at 6 p.m. Meanwhile Elijah quickly arranged things from his end, getting Mike Christianson, his longtime staffer and old law school friend, to be his best man and securing a Baltimore judge as our officiant. By the time I arrived back at the airport, he picked me up and everything was in place at the house. My "wedding dress" was a pantsuit—eggshell blue—what I had worn to speak in Atlanta that day. We were married in the living room—Callie, Gary, and their little baby; Mike and his wife, Jean; and the officiant and his wife—if you count the baby, we had seven witnesses or guests. That was it. That was Elijah being romantic. Honest, simple, straightforward, planned in morning, done by evening. In his own way, so sweet. Or as he likes to say, "effective and efficient."

Why didn't we have a large wedding or a big celebration? First, we were older than most brides and grooms. And there was the age difference between us—almost twenty years—which probably mattered to other people more than it did to us. But mostly we were sensitive to the feelings of others in the family. Elijah sought to spare others who had been hurt by divorce and separation any mixed emotions. His daughters, Jennifer and Adia, were very important to Elijah. So were his brothers and sisters and his parents. So we didn't have a big wedding. But what we had was an important new start. Several years later Elijah surprised me by arranging a recommitment ceremony over the Christmas holiday. This was also at the house, but this time I wore a white gown and he wore a tuxedo and we were able to share our love with a larger group of family and friends.

ELIJAH AND I shared a lot and we taught each other a lot. We had what might be called parallel careers, mine in political strategy and policy advocacy, his on the streets and in the halls of

Congress. So, of course, we talked business a lot at home, especially when it was just the two of us. We had a common value system, a common agenda for our community and our country. I became one of his closest advisors, and he mine. What's fascinating is that we arrived at our common vision coming from very different places.

Elijah grew up the child of laborers and preachers, in segregated neighborhoods, in poverty and prejudice. I grew up a "military brat," moving all over the country and the world—Texas, California, Mississippi, Washington State, Oklahoma, Illinois, even Greece—not affluent, but always with a sense of security. We had a roof over our heads, health care, good education, and lived in integrated communities.

But our history was more similar once you scratched the surface. I'm fourth generation from slavery on my mother's side. My great-grandmother was held in slavery as a child. Elijah was not only the child of sharecroppers, but he had told me that only two generations back, his great-grandfather was also a slave. I did not experience the Jim Crow South, but my parents taught it to us through stories about their upbringing, lessons my siblings and I never forgot. It was part of my education, of my fabric. I was in the first generation born in the post–civil rights movement era. But my parents reminded us how they went through racially segregated, supposedly "separate but equal" schools, sat in designated seats at the movies or on the bus, and drank out of "colored" water fountains. Elijah's Baltimore City stories of segregated schools, pools, and stores were so similar. My parents told stories of the negro schools in rural Texas being closed by the white superintendent so that black kids could pick cotton in season. My parents taught me not only the promise of what America could offer, but the pain of what they endured.

Elijah and I came from different places and times, but we came from the same heritage, the same roots. We had the same commitment to making sure we build a society that works for everyone, not just for some. Sure, like any couple, we talked about what to have for dinner, or the weather, or the potholes on our streets, or who would pick up the laundry, but we shared our passion and our purpose—to make life better for people. That's a powerful bond most couples don't have. That's what we talked about at the end of a workday. Or on a rare day off. Or many times when Elijah was ill and resting, or supposed to be resting.

Elijah became increasingly sick over the summer of 2019. He was in and out of the hospital; he was weak; he was under treatment, as he had been many times before. We had no idea that this time would be different.

To understand the entire, long, arduous struggle, we really have to go back, back to the original diagnosis in 1994, when he was told he had thymic cancer, back before I even knew him. It's rare, very rare, and it is almost always fatal. The cancer invades the thymus gland, which produces white blood cells to fight infection. So, it puts the patient in a vulnerable situation immediately. Successful treatment is almost as rare as the disease. In fact, he told me later, when it was found, the doctors gave him six months to live. The five-year survival rate is less than 50 percent. By the time he told me about it, I was "hooked on Elijah." It wasn't a discussion or a decision—are you up for this? By then, I was all in.

He recounted the whole story, how he'd made it past the early hurdles of the disease, going alone to the Mayo Clinic for surgery, radiation, and chemo, and how he did better than everyone expected. Everyone except Elijah. He thought he could just fight it, over and over, and keep battling it back, even if he was losing a little ground each time. Maybe, maybe he could do it again. Maybe not.

The cancer haunted him like a ghost. Just when he was in a good spell, it would return. He would fight back. It would return. Sometimes absent but never gone. That was the pattern. There had even been a recurrence just before our wedding in 2008, but true to form, or bending to Elijah's will, he rallied; he inched his way back; we got married; and we returned to a semi-normal life.

Then came the heart problem in the spring of 2017. We knew Elijah's health had been failing. He was short of breath and his lower legs were so swollen the pores of his skin opened up and wept. He started wearing larger tennis shoes with Velcro straps to accommodate his constantly swollen feet. Our ritual every morning included binding his legs and feet with specialty compression stockings to try to manage the swelling. Doctors at George Washington Hospital told us that Elijah's heart valve wasn't working properly and he needed emergency surgery. It turned out that the world's expert on the transcatheter aortic valve replacement (TAVR) procedure Elijah needed was Dr. Jon Rodney Resar, a cardiologist at Johns Hopkins Hospital, not far from our home.

We scheduled an appointment with Dr. Resar and he explained the procedure. They would replace the valve using a catheter inserted through the groin and then snaked up to the heart. The challenge in Elijah's case was to manage the procedure without exacerbating his other health issues. At one point, Dr. Resar held up a copy of the pig tissue valve and asked me how much I thought it would cost. I knew it had to be expensive, so I guessed $35,000. Dr. Resar looked surprised so I figured I must have been in the ballpark. It was $30,000. That little pig tissue valve cost as much as most automobiles!

This time there was no hiding the situation from the public. He needed the procedure and he needed it now. Elijah and his staff debated whether to release a statement before or after the surgery. The decision was made to issue a carefully worded press announcement immediately after the procedure was completed. Recovery following the procedure was only supposed to take a few days. But what if he had complications on the operating table? What if he didn't survive? Two versions of the announcement were prepared in advance, depending on the surgery outcome. Fortunately, it was successful and the expectation was that he would be up and about soon. But that's not what happened.

Elijah had a major gout attack after the heart surgery. The gout pain was resistant to treatment, affected every joint in his body at once, and even twisted his fingers. He'd never experienced anything like it previously. That attack kept him in the hospital for months instead of days. Elijah was so weakened that he had to undergo in-hospital rehabilitation just to regain the ability to walk. I was still running my D.C.-based consulting firm and nonprofit, but I was less and less available to my team. I had become Elijah's chief medical advocate and companion in the hospital, along with my physician sister, who, at Elijah's request, flew into town for the initial surgery and regularly spoke with his doctors. We stayed in the hospital week after week and developed a new weekday routine: I slept in the room with him each night, went home to shower in the morning, commuted to work each day, then returned in the early evening to have dinner and talk. On weekends, I was there around the clock.

Elijah finally got out of the hospital and was recovering at home. He walked slowly with effort but could not make it up the stairs. So we moved a rented medical bed into our living room and ordered supplies, meds, everything he needed. He slept and worked from there. Medicare-subsidized home health aides helped with his rehabilitation. Elijah regained his strength and eventually returned to work.

Meanwhile, I had been approached about running for governor of Maryland in the spring but deferred considering it until it looked like we were through Elijah's health crisis. His return to work allowed me to think more carefully about my career and about how I might have greater impact. The limitations of working in the nonprofit world in the era of Donald Trump frustrated me. My mother's death in 2015 and Elijah's more recent health challenges reinforced that life was short and that I'd better act with greater urgency.

Elijah and I discussed the opportunity to run for governor. He cautioned me about the dangers of politics and suggested I talk about it with our pastor, Dr. Walter Scott Thomas Sr., who is also a certified life coach, for counseling. Dr. Thomas parked me in front of a whiteboard where he drew charts and graphs and grilled me on what I knew about Maryland politics and policy. After a long session, he concluded that, if it was what I wanted, I should pursue it. I went home and discussed it with Elijah. And I'm sure he and Dr. Thomas also debriefed directly.

Although deeply concerned about the hazards of electoral politics and what my involvement would mean for both of us, Elijah offered his support for my run. I don't know that he loved the idea, but I think he consented because he loved me and he didn't want to block a path that may lead toward my greater purpose.

I took an unpaid leave of absence from my organization and launched my campaign for governor in the fall of 2017, the first African-American woman ever to run for governor of Maryland. I traveled the state and spoke to audiences about my plans for inclusive growth. But I was only in the race three months before Elijah's health took a turn for the worse.

During the last week of 2017, Elijah woke up one night sweating profusely. He needed to go to the bathroom but he could not walk. I shouldered his weight and tried to help him get there. It took us what seemed like hours to travel the ten feet from the bed to the restroom and back. Something was very wrong. We called his primary care physician, Dr. Steve Sisson, and he instructed us to come to the hospital and Elijah was admitted again. New Year's Day 2018 came and went as we awaited word about what it could possibly be. It turned out that Elijah's previous surgery and stint in the hospital had left him susceptible to infection. They could not yet determine the source of the infection but the bacteria from the infection had settled in his left knee. The doctors performed two surgical procedures on his left knee, intended to flush out the bacteria, but instead of improving the situation, it went from bad to worse.

Elijah was never able to walk on his own again. Once it became clear that he would need to remain in the hospital to recover, I dropped out of the gubernatorial race to be his support. Like last time, his hospital stay turned into weeks and then months. Like last time, he was in deep pain much of the time. Our routine was similar, but things were different this time. Elijah was different. He was in constant pain and seemed to recognize that life would never be the same.

I shut down my D.C. office and became his primary caretaker/political confidante/partner. Eventually, slowly Elijah made his way back to work, but very much compromised. He had to use a walker or a scooter, had to be helped in and out of the car, and up and down stairs. He limited his office hours, did as much by phone as possible, and appeared on the House floor or in front of the media only when absolutely necessary. But he never cut back on his commitment to work on the Hill. And he was a vocal champion for the 2018 midterm elections, telling Americans that it was imperative for voters to flip the House from Republican to Democrat, to place checks and balances on President Trump's power.

Elijah Cummings's approach was steadfast: new valve, old cancer, bad knee, gout—they were simply realities to be reckoned with. Just keep going. So we did.

THANKFULLY, THE DEMOCRATS regained the majority in the midterms. Elijah was the chairman of the Committee on Oversight and Reform. It was a joyous day in early January 2019 when Elijah was sworn in and accepted the gavel, and gave a speech to a crowd of supporters, family, and friends in the committee hearing room. Elijah was finally in a position to lead investigations and to set the agenda for hearings. But he was sober about the realities of the threats he and his committee would face from the Trump administration and congressional Republicans. Despite his pain, he threw himself into his work.

Then, in late summer, just before his speech at the National Press Club, he took yet another bad turn. He was readmitted to Johns Hopkins and diagnosed with pneumonia. But the underlying suspicion was that the cancer had come back. Elijah was weaker than I'd seen him in years. A day before he was to give the speech, I asked if he intended to do it. That's when he said, "Maya, I'll be there if I have to crawl." He had a sense his fate was written and his time was limited.

He was given a four-hour pass from the hospital to give the talk. But Elijah was so drained from the illness and the ordeal of the trip that when his aides maneuvered him to the podium, pale and unsteady, I thought he might drop. Then he looked at the crowd, four or five times the size of what had been expected two months before when he'd been invited, before his investigations into the administration, before the shootings in Dayton and El Paso, and before Trump's twitter attack on Baltimore and Elijah. He looked at the crowd and you could see him become energized. He stood up for his beloved city, district, and country. He exhorted the audience to listen and, more important, to take action. He was passionate as only Elijah Cummings could be. The gathering of usually callous Washington media cheered and gave him a standing ovation.

Exhausted and barely able to keep going, he went straight back to the hospital. He was released a few days later when the pneumonia cleared. During the next few weeks, he managed to continue vital work. He was on the phone with Nancy Pelosi, Adam Schiff, Jerry Nadler, and his staff. He read testimony. He reviewed the impeachment updates. He signed subpoenas.

So many times, I said, "Elijah, that's enough for today."

"Okay, I'll stop soon," he'd say. Often his exhaustion would just force him to close his eyes for a while.

During this time, doctors at Hopkins and NIH monitored the state of his cancer. It was obviously recurring; the question was, could they do anything to slow it down, or limit it. New growths appeared on his kidneys and liver. We explored the possibility of ablating the lesions and starting a new drug. After years of being in borderline function, his kidneys had finally failed. So he began three-times-a-week dialysis visits.

Earlier, in December 2018, I had run for and won the job of chair of the Maryland Democratic Party, a volunteer but demanding position. I tried to do what Elijah would do. Do it all—somehow fulfill my obligations to the job while giving Elijah full-time care, as I had done in the past. But this time was different. The care-giving was 24/7. It was so overwhelming that we asked his family members to help out. And once it became crystal clear that we were nearing the end, I stopped doing the work of the Maryland Democratic Party to be with Elijah around the clock.

We all did everything we could. But it wasn't long before his dialysis treatment routine just wasn't working. The doctors said Elijah needed surgery to install a fistula to aid in the dialysis process but then they determined his body couldn't handle it. Instead of conducting the procedure, they readmitted him to Johns Hopkins. He never came out of the hospital again.

There became—I think the best word is an "inevitability"—to it. He knew and I suspected we were coming to the end. We didn't know when or how but it was coming, as if you could see it like a train approaching in the distance, when you're not sure how far away it is but you know it is steadily coming toward you. That's when he began to talk differently. He would say he was tired, no matter how much rest he got, just tired all the time. He complained of constant pain. It was clearly physical, but it was also emotional and spiritual. The inner Elijah was burning out.

That's when he called his chief of staff, Vernon Simms, and asked for the "envelope." When Elijah had gone in for the TAVR two years earlier, he had given two envelopes to Vernon: one, a list of people to call if all went well in the procedure, the other, for his chief to give to me if he did not survive the procedure. Of course, he made it through the TAVR and I never saw the second envelope. Vernon tried several times to give it back to Elijah but he wouldn't take it. Now he asked Vernon to make sure he gave me the envelope. At first Vernon told Elijah not to worry about getting the envelope to me, that the congressman would rally as he always had.

But Elijah said to Vernon, "I'm tired. I'm just so tired. I have to get out of here. I'm too tired."

Vernon asked to talk to me and he asked, "Does he mean that he's tired and wants to get out of there, out of the hospital, to go home and rest? Or does he mean something else?"

"Something else," I said. I handed the phone back to Elijah and Vernon assured him he would give the envelope to me.

We knew he was dying but that was as close as we got to uttering the words. We talked about the past, what Elijah had done, and about the future, and all that remained to be done. But we did not use the word "death." We just knew.

Then, a day or so later, the doctors came in and told us, "The cancer has spread to his upper thigh, gluteal muscles, and into his bones and there is, sadly, nothing more we can do." No treatments, no procedures, no drug trials, nothing. Elijah asked to be moved to hospice care the same day. I quickly checked out two options, then decided which would work best and we moved him into the facility at nine that evening. There was no prediction as to how long he might be there, how long he had. Less than six hours later, he was gone. I thought we would have more time to talk, reflect, and say good-bye. I was inconsolable.

Vernon gave me the envelope the next day. Elijah had spelled out everything: the details of his funeral, where it was to be held, who would speak, which suit he wanted to be buried in, what songs should be sung, everything. And I followed it to the letter. But his family and I wanted him to receive the respect he deserved since he had been so disrespected by Trump in the months leading up to his death. So we worked with Speaker Pelosi's office and staff at the U.S. Capitol to arrange for him to lie in state.

On October 24, 2019, at the National Statuary Hall, Elijah Cummings was the first African-American member of Congress to receive that tribute. His flag-draped casket was carried by an honor guard of military pallbearers. The Morgan State Choir sang. I stood by his casket. Leaders of both Democrats and Republicans came to pay him homage. Senate minority leader

Chuck Schumer said, "His authority came not from the office he held, nor from the timbre of his voice. It came from the moral force of his life." House Speaker Nancy Pelosi called him "our North Star" and "a mentor of the House." House majority leader Steny Hoyer spoke of him as "a calming influence in a sea of rage" after the Freddie Gray incident. Republican congressman Mark Meadows talked about their "unexpected" friendship; "for those of us who know Elijah, it is not unexpected or surprising." Senate majority leader and Republican Mitch McConnell praised him, as others of both parties paid their respects, including Vice President Pence, Attorney General William Barr, former governor of Maryland Martin O'Malley, Mayor Jack Young, and members of the Congressional Black Caucus, which Elijah had once led.

One day later, on October 25, at the New Psalmist Baptist Church in Baltimore, almost five thousand people gathered—from the highest offices of government to plain folks from Baltimore neighborhoods, admirers and adversaries, Republicans and Democrats, black, brown, and white, old and young, close friends and family, and total strangers—any and all who felt the loss of Elijah Cummings. Elijah was honored and eulogized by many, including Speaker Pelosi, President Clinton, President Obama, Secretary Clinton, former head of the NAACP Kweisi Mfume, staff aide Harry Spikes, Elijah's brother James, his pastor Bishop Walter Scott Thomas, his daughters, Jennifer and Adia, and me.

I tried to write what I would say but I could not. I thought and I prayed. As Elijah would do, I waited for God to speak to me. I thought about what he would have wanted me to say. When I stood in front of that gathering, the words came. I spoke from my heart, from my soul, about the finest man and most beautiful spirit I have ever known. I let my passion and love for Elijah speak and sing. I said good-bye to my Elijah.

That was not the end. Not quite. There were still two important decisions to be made. One was a decision I had to make for Elijah, without Elijah, to try to do what he would want. Do we carry his book to completion? The writing was largely done. Do we finish what he had begun, or rather, what we had begun? I had been an advocate for the book for a long time, years actually. More than a year earlier, I had started searching for a writer to work with Elijah, and had even taken a pass at it personally, but I fired myself, realizing that I was much too close to the subject. Then, by happenstance, a friend put me in touch with our writer/collaborator, Jim Dale. Elijah and Jim connected immediately. Through another friend, I connected with a publisher for the project. Once Elijah and Jim began, the plan was for the two of them to work on the book throughout 2019. The book would then be published the following spring, at which time, between his duties in Washington, Elijah would go on the news media circuit to share his stories and his legacy. But now he has left us. What should be done? Should the book be closed, literally? Or would he still want it to reach the people he so desperately wished to inspire and provide with hope and passion, those future generations he spoke of so often? I thought about what he would say if he were here to speak. I knew there was only one answer for Elijah Cummings: *"Finish what you started!"* It was one of his mantras, words of advice he often gave people. He felt that completing the job, any job or task, was a sign of integrity—a value he believed that was too often lacking in society. This book you are holding in your hands is what he wanted to express to the world.

Then there was the other decision. A personal one for me. Over the past few months, several times, he said to me, "Maya, you should take my seat in the House" or "You would be good in my seat." Not wanting to contemplate him not being here, I would always brush it off and say there was no need to think about that; he was in the seat and would be forever. But he would come back to the subject. In the days after his death, as he would have done, I thought hard about it, I prayed, I talked to a handful of people I truly trust. And despite the loss I was experiencing and the fact that I had other pressing health concerns on the horizon, I knew that running for his seat was the right thing to do.

On November 11, 2019, I gave an interview to the *Baltimore Sun* and went on the Rachel Maddow show on MSNBC to make my announcement. I talked about Elijah's dreams and legacy and our work together. "I've been on this path of fighting for the soul of our democracy. . . . And he wanted me to continue this fight, and I'm going to continue this fight and run the race, and prayerfully, win." I revealed another decision I had made, also made with Elijah. In the next few days, I would be going in for a preventative double mastectomy. My mother had died of breast cancer; my sister had been diagnosed with it; and Elijah had urged me, over and over, to take this step to save my life. He said that I was always focused on others and it was time for me to take care of myself. In fact, he and I had attended the consultation with the breast surgeon together and I had scheduled it weeks before. Hearing Elijah's voice in my head, I was determined to go through with it even as I campaigned to keep the flame of his work burning.

As soon after the surgery as I could, I returned to work—as Elijah would have done. As a former congressional aide and longtime political operative, I was always up on the work in our district, voter needs, health and safety issues, the Oversight Committee, and progress of the impeachment process—it was our dinner table and phone conversation. In those last days of his illness, his passing, and my announcement, events had occurred at blinding speed: the whistle-blower, the Ukraine/Zelensky phone call, the accusation of trading aid for political dirt, Giuliani's involvement, Secretary of State Mike Pompeo's role, Mick Mulvaney's admission that aid was withheld (and his breathtaking statement that people should "get over it"), Ambassador Sondland's confirmation of a "quid pro quo" deal, the House resolution on formal impeachment inquiry, Giuliani business associates implicated, Schiff's announcement of public hearings, former secretary of state John Bolton dangling more evidence, Trump administration officials including Russia advisor Fiona Hill and Lieutenant Colonel Alexander Vindman and diplomat Bill Taylor providing damning testimony.

As if sped by his passing, events moved even faster in the days just after Elijah's death. On December 18, 2019, Speaker Nancy Pelosi banged the gavel and announced that the House of Representatives voted 230 to 197 to impeach President Donald J. Trump, the third president in the history of the United States to face impeachment charges. That evening, during her press conference, she spoke about Elijah, saying that he "isn't with us physically in this room, but I know [he] is present, was present all day for the deliberations." She honored him as a key force in the inquiry, "our North Star." And she quoted him, "When the history books are written about this tumultuous era, I want them to show that I was among those in the House of Representatives who stood up to lawlessness and tyranny." She added, "He also said, somewhat presciently, 'When we're dancing with angels, the question will be, "What did you do to make sure we kept our democracy intact?"'" We did all we could, Elijah. We passed the two articles of impeachment. The president is impeached."

As the year neared its end, on December 28, 2019, the *Baltimore Sun* posthumously awarded Elijah Cummings the Person of the Year in Maryland. The editorial board's recognition referred to Elijah's own words, again: "'When we're dancing with the angels,' he said at a hearing in February, 'the question will be asked: "In 2019, what did we do to make sure we kept our democracy intact? Did we stand on the sidelines and say nothing?"'" The *Sun* story concluded, "Though he couldn't have known the angels would come for him before the year was out, Elijah Cummings certainly must have been secure in the knowledge that he did all he could to stand up for his beliefs. We are."

A day later, in their year-end feature "The Lives They Lived," the *New York Times Magazine* recognized a select group of "artists, innovators and thinkers we lost in the past year." Writer Astead Herndon concluded his profile of Elijah with these words: "He always knew that democracy and racism were ideas in direct conflict, and that perfecting one required overcoming the other."

Two weeks into the new year, on January 15, 2020, Speaker

Pelosi marked the presentation of the articles of impeachment, saying, "[T]he House of Representatives upheld its constitutional duty and voted articles of impeachment against the President of the United States, Donald Trump. . . . So sad, so tragic for our country that the actions taken by the President to undermine our national security, to violate his oath of office and to jeopardize the security of our elections, the integrity of our elections, has taken us to this place. . . . So today, we will make history. When the Managers walk down the hall, we will cross a threshold in history, delivering articles of impeachment against the President of the United States for abuse of power and obstruction of the House. As we make that history, we are making progress for the American people, progress in support of our Constitution and progress in honor of the sacrifice and the vision of the Founders, progress and honor of the sacrifice of the men and women in uniform, and progress for the future of our children. Make it very clear that this President will be held accountable, that no one is above the law. . . .

"I am very honored to be here with our six chairmen who worked so hard to help us to uphold the Constitution with their legislating, their investigating, their litigating: . . . Chairman of the Judiciary Committee, Jerry Nadler; Mr. Schiff, Chairman of the House Committee on Intelligence; Congresswoman Maxine Waters, Chair of the Financial Services Committee, and Congresswoman Carolyn Maloney, Madam Chair of the Oversight Committee; Congressman—and Mr. Chairman—Eliot Engel of the Foreign Affairs Committee, and Richie Neal, Chairman of the Ways and Means Committee."

Then, one more time she echoed the soul-stirring and indelible words of Elijah, "And we honor our darling Elijah Cummings, who said that 'one day when we are dancing with the angels, what will we say about what we did at this difficult time in our country's history?'"

Led by the House clerk and the House sergeant at arms, Speaker of the House Nancy Pelosi and the managers formally presented the articles of impeachment to the secretary of the Senate. It was a little more than one year from the date that Congressman Elijah Cummings became chair of the Oversight and Reform Committee of the House of Representatives. Oversight had been carried out. Reform was the remaining goal.

So much of this had begun with Elijah's work—the hearings and investigations of the Oversight Committee, the testimony of Trump's personal attorney/fixer Michael Cohen, subpoenas for White House documents and financial records, court cases to compel cooperation where the administration had been stonewalling, the stirring, inspiring, passionate words to Congress and the country, and the promises to our children.

So much happened after his death. The impeachment trial ended with an acquittal in the Senate. There were brief hopes that Republicans of conscience might stand up to Majority Leader Mitch McConnell and the wrath of Trump but those flames were snuffed out, predictably and quickly. The outcome would have come as no surprise to Elijah. He had been reluctant to pursue impeachment in the first place because he was well aware of the president's willingness to go to any lengths to bury the truth.

Then came something unexpected: the novel coronavirus. While the pandemic was not Trump's doing, it was a global threat that world health organizations and our own CIA had warned the president about in January 2020. From the outset, the president attempted to undermine its truth. First, he and his allies at Fox News claimed it was the Democrats' new hoax. Then he promised it would disappear, like "a miracle." He said Democrats were exaggerating it. He minimized its impact, even as the cases and deaths in the United States mounted. Of course he blamed others: he divided humanity, calling it the "Chinese virus." He said we should go back to work and life because our economy was more important than saving lives. He then attempted to say his early inaction was due to his distraction over his impeachment.

Experts estimate that thousands and perhaps hundreds of thousands of people in the United States will likely die from this disease. And early data has shown that the coronavirus is markedly more devastating to people of color, for reasons of health-care access, or economics, or vulnerability to other compromising illnesses. If God had not taken him first, Elijah himself, who suffered from asthma, hypertension, and cancer, would likely not have survived the coronavirus. In speaking to challenging times, Elijah used to say that the question is not whether we will get through this—because we will get through this—but how we will come out on the other side.

Will we finally decide it's unacceptable and immoral to leave anyone without access to health care or lifesaving prescription drugs? Will we ensure that all of our children have the tools and technology they need to learn both at school and at home?

Will we make sure that hourly and gig-economy workers— many of whom have been deemed essential in the coronavirus crisis—are able to earn a living wage and have the benefits their families need? Will we house the homeless?

These were the concerns and principles that Elijah and I believed in and fought for before the crisis. They are priorities that I included in my new platform of HOPE—Healthy and safe communities, Opportunities for youth, Prosperous families, and Economic justice—for the Seventh Congressional District.

This crisis, despite its human devastation, can leave a positive imprint, but only if we build the public and political will to turn our values and priorities toward policies that uplift all humanity, especially the marginalized. We will only get there if we prioritize what Elijah Cummings saw as a first-order value: the truth.

On February 27, 2020, Speaker Pelosi and Chairwoman Carolyn Maloney, the new chair of the Government Oversight and Reform Committee, designated the committee's hearing room in the Rayburn House Office Building as the Elijah E. Cummings Room. With that act, Elijah became the first African American lawmaker in history to have a room named for him anywhere in the United States Capitol complex. As I watched his colleagues unveil the sign that would grace the entrance to the room, I was both heartened and saddened to see them honoring Elijah's work while knowing he would never see so much of it come to fruition. As I often told people in the days after his death, Elijah's death wasn't just my loss, it was our loss as a nation, and we all have the responsibility to move his legacy forward. Because we know that with every transgression, every disregard for the Constitution, every attempt to act above the law, every denial of truth, our democracy is endangered. That's why in the months and years ahead we must continue to hear Elijah's voice: "We're better than this. We're better than this." Yes, we are. We must be.

Farewell to Elijah Cummings

Selected Excerpts of Eulogies for Elijah Cummings

BISHOP WALTER SCOTT THOMAS
—Elijah's Pastor

Elijah was my friend for almost forty years. He sat right over there. . . . Elijah's last official Congressional act was to sign some subpoenas. I saw him that morning, I did not know he was still working but he was. But that was not his last official act for God. . . . Elijah's last official act for the kingdom of God was to bring power to church. . . . His last official act [takes] place today. . . . The decision was made by his wife that his service would be in one place, the New Psalmist Baptist Church. And he was bringing power to church.

. . . He would be the first to tell you he wasn't perfect . . . that he struggled and wrestled like everybody else . . . that he had to climb the rough side of the mountain. . . . Elijah said I come to church because . . . He looks beyond my faults and God sees my needs. . . . I come to church because I can recognize my failures and I can claim my possibilities so that when I leave . . . I can go out of here and help somebody else.

. . . Elijah brought you to church today so that the moral compass can be reset, so you can get your grounding back, so we can remember "We hold these truths to be self-evident, that all men are created equal and are endowed by their creator with certain inalienable rights of which are life, liberty, and the pursuit of happiness."

. . . Elijah never forgot his grounding. Elijah was like the prophet Elijah . . . according to an Old Testament scholar. . . . Elijah's . . . voice would rise, his lips would quiver, he would say "Come on now, we can do better than this." Elijah said as long as God gives me breath, I will speak for those who cannot speak.

. . . Sleep on Elijah, sleep on. It took me a while to get here but I can stand before my God and I can hear him say, *well done.*

HILLARY CLINTON

—Former Secretary of State

It is no coincidence, is it, that Elijah Cummings shared a name with an Old Testament prophet, whose name, in Hebrew, is "the Lord is my God" . . . who used the power and the wisdom that

God gave him to uphold the moral law that all people are subject to. And because all people are equal, like the prophet, our Elijah could call down fire from heaven. But he also prayed and worked for healing. He weathered storms and earthquakes, but never lost his faith. Like that Old Testament prophet, he stood against corrupt leadership of King Ahab and Queen Jezebel, and he looked out for the vulnerable among us. . . . And he kept reminding us . . . the American people want to live their lives without fear of their leaders.

Elijah often said his philosophy was simple: do something, go out and do something. No matter how daunting a problem seems, no matter how helpless you feel, surely there is something you can do. . . . You can defend the truth, you can defend democracy, you can lift up others.

Toward the end of his life he said, "I am begging the American people to pay attention to what is going on, because if you want to have a democracy intact for your children and your children's children and generations yet unborn, we have got to guard this moment. This is our watch."

NANCY PELOSI

—*Speaker of the House*

Elijah Cummings [was] the first African-American lawmaker ever to lie in repose in the Capitol of the United States. . . . Elijah brought people together in life of different parties and in his death of different parties.

. . . As we know from the Old Testament, there is a tradition to leave a seat at the table for Elijah, who might show up, but our Elijah always made a seat at the table for others. He made a seat at the table for children who needed an education, for even new members of Congress so that he could mentor them, for all who wanted to be part of the American dream.

. . . God truly blessed America with the life and legacy of Elijah E. Cummings, mentor, Master of the House, North Star, Mr. Chairman. May he rest in peace, Elijah Cummings.

KWEISI MFUME
—Former Head of the NAACP

Elijah and I spent a lot of time in the last couple of years privately just talking about our own lives, our own death . . . our own mortality, our own funerals. Whether he was going to go before me or I was going to go before him. [I'd say] because I was three years older than Elijah . . . I will probably be leaving before you. And he would say . . . I hear they're all filled up downstairs, where you're going—where you're going, you may have to get in line.

Sometimes out of the blue, he would call me and just speak [and say] . . . you have turned forty. Of course, Elijah was thirty-seven. Like [when I] turned sixty and of course, he was fifty-seven. . . . Yesterday was my birthday and I did not hear from my friend Elijah.

. . . My preference would be for Elijah to be standing here right now.

JENNIFER CUMMINGS
—*Elijah's Older Daughter*

Daddy . . . here's a letter to express my gratitude to you for a life-time of lessons, and memories and blessings. Dear Dad . . . while you were congressman and Mr. Chairman and a seasoned political leader, perhaps the most important title you held in your sixty-eight years of life on this earth was "Dad."

Thank you for loving me before I even took my first breath in this world. I remember you telling me how when I was born, you were amazed you could hold me in the palm of your hand—just one hand, my life in your hands.

Thank you for teaching me the dual power of my beauty and my brilliance. This might sound boastful . . . but ever since I was a little girl, my dad always told me I was beautiful. . . . Dad wanted me to understand and appreciate my blackness. And truly feel that my rich brown skin was just as beautiful as alabaster or any shade of the rainbow. . . . So I could truly appreciate myself and what may be different, from the width of my nose to the fullness of my lips and the coarseness of my hair. . . . I vividly remember being on the playground . . . a classmate called me ugly. . . . I retorted, "Well, my daddy says I'm beautiful."

. . . Thank you Dad, for . . . teaching me to be bold and confident . . . to stand up against bullies. . . . Thanks for teaching me what leadership means. Thank you for teaching me to persevere.

. . . I will miss our brief conversations between meetings and hearings. And I will miss our longer ones. Our conversations will not be in person anymore, but they will be just as they have always been—filled with spirit and soul. I love you, Dad.

ADIA CUMMINGS

—*Elijah's Younger Daughter*

You all will have to forgive me, I'm reading from my phone. I am a millennial after all.

. . . It means a lot to our family to know how loved my father was by his community and colleagues.

. . . My sister and I were fortunate enough to hold the highest honor, which was being able to call him "Dad." And I would be remiss if I didn't share a glimpse of what it was like to be his daughter.

. . . Whenever I'd call, he'd answer "Hey, Beautiful," and I could tell that he was happy to hear from me. He was never hesitant to give his opinion, whether asked for or not, and was quick to remind me, at any given moment, that I owed him some money. He wasn't a father known for his patience, but rather for his persistence. When I was getting ready to take my driving test, he had me parallel park, what felt like fifty times in a row, until I got it down to a science. . . . I passed my test on the first try.

. . . Last year I gave him a card for Father's Day that said, "A parent's job is to see their child the way God sees them, and you do." And I would encourage all the parents here, and watching, to see their children the way my dad saw me, the way God sees me. Without limitations, not bound by obstacles or circumstances, and with the power to determine my own destiny.

JAMES CUMMINGS
—*Elijah's Brother*

Elijah was my older brother by three years. I can tell you . . . at times it was easy, and at other times it was not. I followed him into middle school and the teachers expected so much of me. When it came time for high school . . . he wanted me to go to City College [high school]. He said . . . it's an all-boys school so you'll have no distraction. I said, "but I love distractions."

. . . Elijah . . . [always] wanted to be in a position to help the people who could not help themselves. . . . I want to thank each and every one of you [for coming]. You can give someone your car, let them borrow it, or your homes, or whatever the case may be. The one thing you cannot get back is time. Each and every one of you have given up hours of your time to honor my brother. And for that I am eternally grateful.

HARRY SPIKES
—*Congressional Staff/District Director*

The remarks that I will give to you today are entitled "The Final Lesson."

The Congressman asked me [to help him out for] one day in D.C. . . . Little did I know that this will turn into . . . years of working with an angel. Suddenly my life changed from District Director to bodyguard, mechanic, advisor, driver, chef . . . most importantly, friend. . . .

He always took time to teach me and the staff valuable life lessons.

Lesson number one: Compassion and kindness . . . He taught me that compassion and kindness brought us closer to God . . . the keys to uniting the human spirit.

Lesson number two: The Congressman believed in bridges . . . that an opportunity, no matter how big or small, made the difference between life or death.

Lesson number three: Value your friendships. Be the foundation for your friends when the house collapses, be the roof for your friends when rain comes.

Lesson number four: . . . a true leader, to get the ball down the court, to win, shares the ball. Give others the opportunity to lead.

Lesson number five: Work through your pain. . . . When we traveled the country, his mission was to fight for the soul of democracy . . . he was always in pain. However, when it was time to address his audience, the Congressman transformed into a spiritual warrior.

For days I've been trying to figure out the . . . final lesson. But I finally got it. The Congressman would tell me, Harry, remember to be greater than your pain. Continue to fight when all hope is lost. . . . If one leg doesn't work, use a walker, at least you will be standing. . . . [R]emember the final lesson— life may change; you may change; hard choices will come. But the Congressman proved to us all that courage and will are timeless.

MAYA CUMMINGS
—*Elijah's Wife*

This man lived for God and he is of God. I have come here today to say two simple words: Thank you. Thank you . . .

I want you all to know that . . . what Congressman, Chairman Cummings did was not easy. And it got infinitely more difficult in the last months of his life. When he sustained personal attacks and attacks on his beloved city. While he carried himself with grace and dignity in all public forums . . . it hurt him. . . . He was a man of soul and spirit. He felt very deeply. He was very empathetic. It was one of his greatest gifts . . . his ability to be a public servant, and a man of the people.

. . . [I]t wasn't easy in the last months of his life because he absolutely was in pain. But . . . he was a walking miracle. Do you know that he was diagnosed with a life-threatening illness more than twenty-five years ago? He was given six months to live more than twenty-five years ago!

. . . It was my distinct honor and privilege to be his spouse. Just two days before he died, he was in a lot of pain. He could no longer walk. And he kept saying, "I'm tired. I'm ready to go."

. . . [T]he wonderful world-class staff at the Johns Hopkins Hospital . . . said that they wanted to give him sunshine therapy . . . so they rolled his entire medical bed out of the room onto the rooftop of Johns Hopkins Hospital. . . . Everywhere the sun was shining, and it was just absolutely glorious. It was God's day. . . . [H]e looked out over the Inner Harbor, Harbor East; he looked toward South Baltimore, his beloved South Baltimore, where he grew up in his early years; he looked toward the downtown; and he looked toward the west side and he said, "Boy, have I come a long way."

And he absolutely came a long way.

. . . Thank you for allowing him to serve you because it was his greatest honor and privilege to work on behalf of all of you.

BILL CLINTON

—*Forty-Second President*

Almost exactly twenty-one years ago Elijah invited me here [to his church] on the Sunday before the election. . . . If you're president, your staff is always trying to tell you why you shouldn't do something. . . . My staff said, I get why you want to go to an African-American church, but why would you want to go to Baltimore—they always vote for you. Why would you go for Elijah Cummings . . . he literally hadn't finished one term yet. . . . I said, I get the feeling this is something we ought to do. I got to listen to Elijah that day . . . his quiet reasoned voice, going into his booming voice—"They who wait upon the Lord will have their strength renewed with wings as eagles."

I've had a lot of chances to think about . . . Elijah's lasting legacy to us. We should think again about the prophet Elijah. He was about to be killed for . . . his faith. [At] Mount Sinai, he received a message from God. Go up and stand on top of the mountain and wait for the voice of God. . . . And a huge wind came . . . then an earthquake . . . then the fire came. Then what does the scripture say—"A still small voice." We should hear Elijah now in the quiet times . . . when we need courage . . . and don't know if we believe anymore. Let our Elijah be for us "a still small voice" that keeps us going. . . .

BARACK OBAMA

—*Forty-Fourth President*

The Parable of the Sower . . . tells us . . . [of] those with a noble and good heart, who hear the word, retain it, and by persevering produce a crop. Elijah Cummings came from good sowers and . . . goodness took root.

. . . His parents were sharecroppers from the South, . . . then sought something better in this city. . . . Robert worked shifts at a plant and Ruth cleaned other people's homes. They became parents of seven, preachers to a small flock. I had the pleasure of meeting Elijah's mother . . . and she told me she prayed for me every day, and I knew it was true. And I felt better for it. Sometimes people say they're praying for you, and you don't know. They might be praying *about* you, but you don't know if they're praying *for* you.

Elijah's example: the son of parents who rose from nothing to carve out just a little something. The public servant who toiled to guarantee the least of us have the same opportunities that he had earned. . . . That's why he fought for justice. . . . That's why he went on to fight for the rights and opportunities of forgotten people all across America, not just in his district.

. . . It's been remarked that Elijah was a kind man. . . . I want my daughters to know . . . that being a strong man includes being kind. That there's nothing weak about kindness and compassion. There's nothing weak about looking out for others. There's nothing weak about being honorable.

. . . [T]he "honorable" Elijah E. Cummings . . . this is a title that we confer on all kinds of people who get elected to public office . . . but Elijah Cummings was honorable before he was elected to office. There's a difference. There's a difference if you were honorable and treated others honorably outside the limelight, on the side of a road, in a quiet moment counseling somebody you work with, letting your daughters know you love them.

As president, I knew I could always count on Elijah being honorable and doing the right thing. And people have talked about his voice. There is something about his voice. . . . I would watch Elijah rally his colleagues. "The cost of doing nothing isn't nothing," he would say, and folks would remember why they entered into public service.

. . . "Our children are the living messengers we send to a future we will never see," he would say, and he would remind all of us that our time is too short not to fight for what's good and what is true and what is best in America. Elijah Cummings was a man of noble and good heart. His parents and his faith planted the seeds of hope and love and compassion and the righteousness and that good soil of his. He has harvested all the crops that he could, for the Lord has now called Elijah home to give His humble, faithful servant rest.

Acknowledgments

From Maya Rockeymore Cummings

"I feel your spirit" were the words Elijah spoke to me more than twenty years ago when we first started getting to know each other in 1998. These words, along with his amazing ability to listen and observe, caused me to believe that he was someone special, a man who would become my best friend, mentor, love, and life partner.

It was only later that I learned that one of Elijah's greatest gifts was that of spiritual discernment. He could literally read people's souls, feel the spirit and mood of a crowded room, and feel the significance of the moment. He always liked to get to an event early, before his speeches, so that he could "feel the room." He then adjusted his remarks to reflect what he felt the people needed.

It was his ability to listen, observe, and feel—his deep empathy—that informed the words in this book. His words are what he felt America needed to hear. He met and spoke with Donald J. Trump on more than one occasion and he took the measure of the man. His book contains a warning to the American people about Mr. Trump's character and what could happen to our democracy if we fail to heed the warning signs and make our electoral decisions accordingly.

I first would like to thank Elijah for everything he poured into me and for sharing the best of himself with me and the world. His longtime friends used to tell me that I made him a better man, but the reality is that he also made me a better woman. We shared so many of the same interests and beliefs that we fed each other's souls. I am immensely grateful that God saw fit for our lives to merge.

Elijah and I spent many months over the last two and a half years of his life in and out of hospitals and doctors' appointments. I would like to give a special thanks to all of the healthcare professionals who helped Elijah throughout this time; including Dr. Stephen Sisson, his primary care physician, and my sister, Dr. Meredith Brooks, whom Elijah asked to be with him during his initial heart valve replacement surgery, and who remained an informal member of his care team for the rest of his life.

I had long wanted Elijah to write a book about his life and spent many years trying to find the right team to help bring his story to fruition. I am profoundly grateful to Amy Elias for introducing me to James "Jim" Dale, the book's collaborator. As soon as Jim and Elijah met, they hit it off and began to go to work almost immediately. Jim, I thank you for the many hours you spent with Elijah, capturing and conveying his words and voice, and shepherding this book to completion.

I thank Tina Sharkey who connected me to her sister, Lisa Sharkey, years ago. This connection ended up leading to this book's publisher, HarperCollins, where Lisa is a senior vice president. I thank the entire HarperCollins team including Lisa Sharkey, Matt Harper, Trina Hunn, and Rachel Elinsky. I thank Elijah's book agent, David Black, for providing the expertise and guidance to seal the book contract deal as well as his insight, advocacy, and advice along the way.

I would like to give a special word of thanks to Speaker Nancy Pelosi, a daughter of Baltimore, who befriended and supported her colleague Elijah, a son of Baltimore. Her guidance, friendship, and support of Elijah was a source of comfort to him and influenced his deep loyalty to her and admiration for her leadership. I am deeply grateful that Speaker Pelosi agreed to write the book's foreword.

I thank my brother, Mark Rockeymoore, for his assistance in helping to flesh out an earlier version of Elijah's story, as well as Wes Moore for providing book-publishing guidance in the early years of this project. I thank Sally Roy and Bob Herbert for their advice on publicizing this book and bringing another aspect of Elijah's life to light through their award-winning documentary *Against All Odds: The Fight for a Black Middle Class.*

I thank all of the dignitaries, staff, and mentees who spoke at Elijah's homegoing service and those who gave permissions for excerpts from their funeral remarks to be included at the end of this book. I thank his incredible staff, his family, and everyone who shared photos and stories to help complete this book. And, although they are both deceased, I thank Elijah's parents for raising this extraordinary man.

Elijah always used to say, "I'm just an ordinary man called to an extraordinary mission." I think Elijah was an extraordinary man with an extraordinary story. I hope you enjoy and take to heart the aspects of his story shared in the pages of this book.

From James Dale

It is hard to list acknowledgments—those who made this book possible—without its simply being a list of one: Congressman Elijah E. Cummings. He made the decision to chronicle his remarkable life story and he made the decision to select me to help tell his story, a singular honor for me.

But if Congressman Cummings tops the list, Maya Rockeymoore Cummings, Elijah's wife, confidante, soulmate, is a close second. My being selected would never have happened without her. Maya was in search of the right person to convey Elijah's legacy and voice. She came to me by way of our mutual acquaintance and good friend, Amy Elias, the "great connector." From there, it came together.

Our editors at HarperCollins were exceptional—truly out of the ordinary—first Lisa Sharkey, senior vice president, who expressed interest in the book to Maya even before there was a book, and then Matt Harper, perhaps the best editor I have ever worked with. My longtime literary agent, David Black, helped us all with his calm reason, his experience, and his wisdom, as did agent Rica Allanic, who worked closely with me throughout.

Congressman Cummings's staff and associates were invaluable, always available, always open and cooperative, always moving my needs, requests, research, and questions to the top of their packed schedules: Jean Waskow, Vernon Simms, Harry Spikes, David Rapallo, Lucinda Lessley, and those behind the scenes. The congressman's daughters, Jennifer and Adia, shared memories and feelings and photographs. Elijah's brothers and sisters opened their albums of family photos as well. There were others, many others, who worked along the way with Elijah, who counted him as a mentor, who were touched by him. They all helped write this book.

And, as always, I thank my wife, Ellen, for being there every day—every day I wasn't available because I was meeting or talking with the congressman, or writing, or rewriting, or editing . . .

This has been the endeavor of a lifetime, a tribute to a great lifetime.

About the Authors

REPRESENTATIVE ELIJAH CUMMINGS was born and raised in Baltimore, Maryland. He obtained his bachelor's degree in political science from Howard University, serving as student government president and graduating Phi Beta Kappa, and then graduated from the University of Maryland School of Law. The congressman served thirteen terms in the House, representing Maryland's 7th congressional district. He also served as the chairman of the Committee on Oversight and Reform until his death in October 2019. His widow, Dr. Maya Rockeymoore Cummings, lives in Baltimore, where she continues the legacy of her late husband.

JAMES DALE has collaborated on a number of books on sports, business, medicine, and life lessons, among other topics. His works include *The Power of Nice* and *Bullies, Tyrants, and Impossible People*, both with agent-negotiator Ron Shapiro; and *Together We Were Eleven Foot Nine* with Hall of Fame pitcher Jim Palmer.